UNIQUE EATS AND EATERIES

OF

CLEVELAND

Library of Congress Control Number: 2018962613
ISBN: 9781681062068

Book Design: Barbara Northcott

Printed in the United States of America
19 20 21 22 23   5 4 3 2 1

UNIQUE EATS AND EATERIES

OF

CLEVELAND

FRAN GOLDEN AND DAVID G. MOLYNEAUX

DEDICATION

This book is dedicated to the late, great John S. Long, who helped put Cleveland's food scene on the map with his excellent reporting in the *Cleveland Plain Dealer*. With his food expertise, quick wit, and generous spirit, he also taught us a thing or two.

CONTENTS

ACKNOWLEDGMENTS

Thank you to researcher Sarah Chatta and contributing writers Marc Bona and Kristan Schiller. Thank you to all the restaurant owners and chefs who make dining in Cleveland such a pleasure not only with their work but also their words. We found a great willingness among creative chefs to talk about what they do and why. Thanks to Nick Urig from Destination Cleveland for always being available to answer our questions.

We live, work, play, and, yes, eat in Cleveland. We tip our hat to the city and with folding money from our wallets to the servers.

INTRODUCTION

We wrote this book to prove that the food and eateries in our venerable Rust Belt city are a lot better than you might expect; in fact, they are even better than we expected.

Restaurants in Cleveland are blessed with local products from expert farmers. The beef is great, with the Certified Angus Beef brand headquartered in Wooster, about sixty miles south of Cleveland. The Ohio Pork Council represents about eight hundred farmers. Corn is the sweetest you'll find anywhere. Restaurants locally, around the country, and beyond buy gourmet produce, such as mini carrots and microgreens from the Chef's Garden, which is about fifty miles west of Cleveland. Milk and butter arrive fresh.

Eaters are evolving. Cleveland was once a meat-and-potatoes town, which speaks of the workers on whose backs this industrial city was built, many of whom arrived from Eastern Europe hungry for a better life and familiar tastes from their former homes. Some of their restaurants still are going strong, such as Sokolowski's University Inn. Many of today's immigrants come from Central America, the Middle East, and Asia. They have brought their tastes, and their eateries are growing.

Michael Symon, Cleveland's celebrity chef, says that when he moved back home in the 1990s, three or maybe four restaurants were doing fine dining. "To see how it has grown is truly amazing," Symon says. "It's continuing to evolve and just keeps on getting more and more exciting. I would like to see Clevelanders embrace more of the ethnic foods." Symon extols the virtues of eating in Cleveland on national TV, including the ABC show *The Chew*, which he cohosted. Food Network and Travel Channel personalities frequently come to the city. Cleveland has made *USA Today*'s 10Best lists—in fact, Collision Bend Brewing Company was named by readers as best brewpub in the United States in 2018.

With old smokestacks from the defunct steel mills adding an element of industrial chic, the city of nearly four hundred thousand people is gaining a reputation as a cool place to visit. The Rock & Roll Hall of Fame sets both a retro and au courant tone. The city's arts scene just keeps getting better. Museums and the Cleveland Orchestra dazzle as world class.

Food has been a major part of the rejuvenation, too, as chefs come to the cuisine stage with bright, new ideas and gain national attention. The recently opened Larder Delicatessen and Bakery, where pastrami is cured with koji, is just one example. It's all part of a stew of life that encourages young entrepreneurs to invest, millennial boomerangs to return, and new residents to move from other locales, some living in glistening new apartment buildings downtown—an area that felt abandoned only a few years ago. The new energy is reflected in the food scene. Cleveland has been recognized as a top ten city for vegan dining.

Though we strayed just outside the border a few times, we concentrated this book on restaurants in the city proper. We do not feature every top restaurant, going instead for places that have a story to tell. Restaurants have helped revitalize neighborhoods, and chefs are repurposing once-abandoned buildings. Creativity is in the air. The whole city feels newly discovered.

Yes, the amazing West Side Market opened in 1912. The Heinen's supermarket chain turns ninety in 2019. Italian market Gallucci's celebrated its centenary in 2012. Polish Boy Sandwiches popped up in the middle of the last century and are today devoured, including by hipsters. Bertman ballpark mustard got its start in 1925. At the same time, Cleveland does, albeit sometimes slowly, embrace food trends. We have ramen and poke and a whole restaurant dedicated to poutine. We have creative folks serving donuts with beer. Thanks to basketball superstar LeBron James and his CNBC show *Cleveland Hustles*, we even have a Cleveland-style bagel.

UNIQUE EATS AND EATERIES
OF
CLEVELAND

ALLEY CAT OYSTER BAR

Seafood and river views on Ohio's North Coast

Built in a glass box on the edge of the left bank of the Cuyahoga River, the Alley Cat Oyster Bar commands an arresting view of the waters that flow past the edge of Cleveland's downtown before emptying into Lake Erie. The bustling seafood restaurant has a delightful coastal atmosphere, with an open dining room, lively bar scene, and viewing decks outside, all focused on the awesome waterfront show that is especially popular from spring deep into fall.

Noted chef and Cleveland restaurateur Zack Bruell decided to open his take on an American oyster bar (with oysters flown in, of course) in 2015 when developers of the city's Flats District agreed to let him build on one of the river's prime viewing spots. Massive French doors open to the river that is not only home to recreational rowers and a plethora of pleasure motorboaters but is also the path for mammoth freighters. Only a stone's throw away, these behemoths make their slow passage past diners along the narrow, twisting Cuyahoga to and from industries just south of the city center.

Bruell's menu is a wide range of raw and prepared seafood, including an extensive oyster list, lobster rolls, clam chowder, fried calamari (with kimchi), grilled octopus (with succotash), lobster tail, crab cakes, ceviche, shrimp-stuffed peppers, shrimp mac & cheese—and burgers and steaks for the meat-eating crowd.

Alley Cat? The story is that the restaurant's name came from Bruell's girlfriend, who once called him a you know what. The restaurant, which sits among other eateries that recently have risen on rebuilt river frontage, is a playful place on the edge of the serious business of manufacturing, industry, and commercial

Left: Alley Cat specializes in seafood, such as fresh oysters from the East Coast.

Right: The restaurant's main entrance is on River Road on the East Bank of the Flats. The west side of the building is a wall of glass facing the Cuyahoga River.

transportation. Lake Erie loading piers are just to the north as is a fascinating, busy railroad bridge. A rare vertical lift known as the Iron Curtain, the 267-foot bridge rises high off the Cuyahoga to allow boaters to and from Lake Erie and then falls to a close for the dozens of daily freight trains (and Amtrak) rumbling between Chicago and the East Coast.

1056 Old River Rd.
216-574-9999
alleycatoysterbar.com

Rejuvenation riverside in the Flats

For centuries, where the crooked Cuyahoga makes its final meander into Lake Erie, in the center of what now is the city of Cleveland, travelers have stopped for a rest and a bite to eat along the river's East Bank.

Native Americans camped, hunted, and fished here. Moses Cleaveland (with an extra "a" in his name) docked here to survey a town for the Connecticut Land Company in 1796. Longshoremen and others associated with the raw materials of industry relaxed here after loading and unloading ships moving coal north across the Great Lakes and iron ore south to Cleveland's steel mills.

John D. Rockefeller set up his first oil refinery (Standard Oil, 1865) in the flat Cuyahoga lowland between the East Side and West Side of the city, which is built on bluffs above the river. Industry fed a growing city but left a residue of air and waters once so polluted that the Cuyahoga River caught fire thirteen times. Images of the last fire in 1969 burned across the country and became a symbol that political historians believe led to passage of the Federal Clean Water Act in 1972.

Today, at the mouth of the Cuyahoga River, where industry and recreation mix, the rejuvenated riverbanks, within walking distance of downtown, are gentrified with new and renovated apartments, offices, and a booming restaurant scene.

Alley Cat Oyster Bar commands one of the best viewing spots on the Cuyahoga River that empties into Lake Erie a few hundred yards to the north—past the hulking railroad bridge known as the Iron Curtain. (Photos courtesy of Zack Bruell Restaurant Group)

COLLISION BEND BREWING COMPANY

Award-winning beer meets West Coast street food

Tables at this spacious artisanal award-winning brewery and full-service restaurant in the Flats District spill outside onto a porch and patio that are prime spots for watching the action from the Left Bank of the busy Cuyahoga River. Housed in the old Watermark Restaurant building that dates to the 1860s, this eatery is special not only because of its location on the river but also because it has a great menu, which is not typical of breweries.

In good weather, when boaters dock to dine, you may sit beneath night skies that tend to move from a mixture of starry clarity to cloud formations buffeted by the winds and temperature changes of the air in and around nearby Lake Erie. Upriver are iron bridges of various designs and the beginning of the Cuyahoga's most dangerous curve, which gave the brewery and restaurant its name. Sometimes it seems that a huge freighter ship will not make the bend, but river records show that collisions actually have been few, and local tugboat captains are ready to help squeeze even the biggest ships around Collision Bend and through a group of historic bridges that date from 1901.

"My goal is for Clevelanders to see the riverside as something more than a summer playground. When the air freezes, the Cuyahoga River continues to run. It's wild looking—like a moonscape, like a movie set. It's also a place with a fascinating history, where the city's business world began; some of that industry, the lifeblood of Cleveland, still hums."
–Chef Zack Bruell, Collision Bend Brewing Company

Left: Dining at Collision Bend Brewing Company beside the Cuyahoga River on a summer evening at dusk, as the sun sets over Lake Erie with bridges of various styles in the background.

Right: Southern California–influenced menu at Collision Bend pairs well with the brewery's artisanal beers and includes several varieties of street tacos. (Photos courtesy of Zack Bruell Restaurant Group)

Action inside the restaurant is much smoother sailing, and it was named in 2018 as the nation's Best Brewpub in *USA Today*'s 10Best Readers' Choice Awards. The emphasis here is on beer flights, food pairings, and communal small plates, say chef Zack Bruell and noted Cleveland brewer Luke Purcell.

"The beer culture in Cleveland is great," says Julian Bruell, Zack's son, who moved back home from New York to be service director for Collision Bend and other restaurants in the Bruell collection. "We talk with guests to learn what they like in food flavors and beer styles."

The menu is filled with what Zack Bruell calls street foods of Southern California. Menu options include Korean pork belly tacos, lamb tamales, popcorn with chicken schmaltz, roasted brussels sprouts, Asian chicken leg stuffed with shiitake mushrooms, roasted eggplant melt, and bread pudding with dried cherry, almonds, coconut, and rum sauce.

Collision Bend Brewing Company has concocted more than a dozen crisp, bright beers and began canning its first beer, Lake Erie Sunset, in summer 2018, starting with three hundred cases of the pale wheat ale.

1250 Old River Rd.
216-273-7879
collisionbendbrewery.com

LAGO RESTAURANT AND WINE BAR

Italian with views of Lake Erie and the Cuyahoga River

We don't include hotel restaurants in this book, but this one, which is more attached to than ensconced in the Aloft Hotel downtown, was a popular Italian restaurant in the Tremont neighborhood starting in 2006. Lago's chef/owner was enticed to move to the East Bank of the Flats as an anchor restaurant in a development with views of both Lake Erie and the Cuyahoga River. The restaurant, in a new building at a different street level than the hotel, reopened in 2013. The restaurant is also connected to the 23-story Ernst & Young tower.

By day, Lago is a popular place for a business lunch and an afternoon gathering spot on its large outdoor veranda that offers views of Lake Erie and the Flats District on both banks of the Cuyahoga River as it empties into the lake (the word *lago* means "lake" in Italian). At night, it's a romantic date-night restaurant. There's a DJ late on Saturdays for dancing.

From Tremont, Chef Fabio Salerno and his wife, Nicole, brought their contemporary and traditional Italian cuisine and an extensive Italian wine list, from which each bottle may be ordered also by the glass or half bottle. The menu ranges from dishes of the Northern Piedmont region to Sicilian-style seafood choices, all inspired by thirty years of Italian cooking and upbringing by the Salerno family. The family makes its own meatballs with beef, veal, and pork; for a taste, stop at Wednesday happy hour, when a meatball is one dollar. Tuesday is half-price bottle of wine night. Try the roasted calamari, pizza with thin flatbread, lobster gnocchi, steaks, and chops. Draft beer is European.

Top left: The bar at Lago, quiet in early afternoon, is lively for happy hour and into the evenings, spilling outside during warmer months. The restaurant's happy hour pizza is among the best in town.

Right: As the weather turns cooler in the fall, Lago adds an element of fire to its patio outside.

Above left: Lago is an upscale, casual and genial restaurant on the East Bank of the Flats.

1091 W. 10th St.
216-862-8065
lagoeastbank.com

LUCA ITALIAN CUISINE

Swanky and sexy ristorante with great city views

In its five years since opening in 2013, Luca Italian Cuisine has established itself as a prime special occasion restaurant, with all the ingredients—menu, service, sophistication, white tablecloths, and one of the best views of the city's downtown. The romantic and glamorous ristorante sits atop the rocky remnants of the historic Superior Viaduct, built in 1878 as Cleveland's first high-level bridge across the Cuyahoga River. The viaduct was closed to traffic in 1923.

Chef Luca Sema and his wife, Lola, met as teenagers in Albania before moving to Cleveland in 1998. Luca earned his cooking credentials in Italy, Spain, and the United States, where he worked in factories by day and restaurant kitchens at night. Lola, who made wine with her family starting at age eight, earned her sommelier certificate in the United States. The restaurant (and recently a second one in the suburb of Westlake) has a big wine collection.

High ceilings and plush décor give the art-filled dining room a swanky look. A woman lounges naked in an arresting painting hanging over the bar, which has a cosmopolitan feel. Open year-round, the covered brick patio offers its own elegance with chandeliers, but the better views are from inside, looking eastward toward downtown.

Knowledgeable waiters guide you through European-style fine dining, with such Northern Italian entrées as wild boar osso buco and the signature Sacchetti al Tartufo Bianco, which consists of pasta purses stuffed with white truffle, pecorino Romano, Parmigiano Reggiano, and ricotta, finished with white truffle cream sauce. Consider also the platters of elegant antipasti, chef favorite black-and-white striped ravioli stuffed with lobster, and tiramisu.

Weekday happy hour from 5:00 p.m. to 7:00 p.m. (often the best way for a first taste at an expensive restaurant) is a worthy experience,

Left: Luca's covered brick patio, with chandeliers, is open for dinner year round.

Right: A Luca specialty is decadent Sacchetti Al Tartufo Bianco, little melt-in-your-mouth pouches of white truffles and ricotta-stuffed pasta in a truffle cream sauce.

with small plates of calamari, whole-grain crostini, caprese salad with fig balsamic, cavatelli Bolognese, and blue mussels sautéed with white wine.

The old Superior Viaduct, hidden away on the west side of the Cuyahoga River, is surrounded by new and renovated apartments. The river wiggles so much through the Flats District that sometimes after crossing a few bridges you are not certain on which side, east or west, your car sits. If lost, just call the restaurant for directions, and don't be intimidated by a full street of parked cars or a sign that says "private." Drive on: A valet will park the car.

2100 Superior Viaduct
216-862-2761
lucacleveland.com

THE GREENHOUSE TAVERN

Chef Jonathon Sawyer's James Beard Award-winning gastropub

Born in Chicago, raised in Cleveland, Jonathon Sawyer was getting a reputation in New York when he decided to return home with his creative food ideas and give his children a better life. Some of his friends thought he was nuts, but in establishing himself as a Rust Belt original, Sawyer has received national recognition, including a James Beard Award for Best Chef: Great Lakes in 2015. You may have seen him on *Iron Chef* or chewing the fat with pal Michael Symon on *The Chew*.

Opened in 2009, his casual Greenhouse Tavern serves extraordinary American gastropub cuisine. While meat is a focus—one of Sawyer's favorite dishes is the waste-not-want-not roasted pigshead with BBQ sauce—he doesn't ignore vegetarians. Many recipes use house-made vinegar, right up the health-conscious alley. Calling himself "vinegar obsessed," Sawyer debuted his latest book, *House of Vinegar*, in 2018.

Greenhouse, which Sawyer runs with his wife and business partner Amelia, occupies a narrow, brick-walled, historic building on trendy East 4th Street. A big bar is downstairs, and a lively crowd sips craft beer on stools and at wooden tables. Ohio-made bikes hang overhead (because Sawyer is also bike obsessed). Dining upstairs in the loft feels a little fancier, while the rooftop deck provides city views. Eating out front on 4th Street makes for great people-

Those who want to show gratitude to the kitchen team are invited to buy them a round of beer for $10, which gives you an opportunity to ring the ship's bell downstairs in the kitchen.

Left: Chef Jonathon Sawyer says he is vinegar obsessed. (Photo courtesy of The Greenhouse Tavern)

Middle: Sawyer's vegetarian ratatouille Nicoise. (Reprinted with permission from House of Vinegar by Jonathon Sawyer, copyright 2018 photography by Peter Larson)

Right: The lively downstairs dining area of the Greenhouse Tavern, with Sawyer's hanging collection of bicycles. (Photo by Allison Grazia)

watching. Get attention yourself in one of the Tavern's "Peace & Love & Pigshead" T-shirts.

In the kitchen, Sawyer uses local products, including farm-fresh produce, foraged items, meats, and grains. He says he's proud of the fact his business has helped Ohio farms grow. He employs a larder master and forager and experiments with smoke, fermentation, and anything else he can get his head around.

Favorites at Greenhouse include rich foie gras steamed clams with butter and a dose of Tavern vinegar and an Ohio lamb burger topped with "stinky cheese" fondue. The beef tartare (with Stadium mustard and fermented relish) and garlicky pommes frites are some of the best you'll find anywhere. Ohio brussels sprouts get special treatment. Sawyer says the reaction he is always going for from diners is "That was f-ing awesome."

The Greenhouse Tavern
2038 E. 4th St.
216-443-0511
thegreenhousetavern.com

LOLA BISTRO

Star chef Michael Symon's fancy 4th Street spot

Michael Symon is Cleveland's most famous celebrity chef, and he got there promoting his love of meat, including at his flagship fine-dining restaurant. Expect special occasion, expense account-type pricing here. In return you'll be at the fanciest place on bustling East 4th Street, the city's trendiest block. Symon has gained national fame for ABC's *The Chew* and is a fixture on Food Network, including winning the title of "Iron Chef."

With his great laugh, exuberance for food, and friendly personality, perhaps he was born to be a star. From a Greek and Sicilian family, he's a favorite local son. Symon, who opened his first restaurant in the Tremont neighborhood more than twenty years ago, has been credited with starting a "Rust Belt Revival" in the food world. While there are other top chefs in Cleveland, including Zack Bruell and Jonathon Sawyer, who have both had a major impact on the city's culinary scene, Clevelanders and visitors play a local version of "Simon Says," as in Symon talking about a local spot on TV and crowds forming. He's a big promoter and influencer in his hometown.

At this location for more than a decade, Lola is sleek, purposely dark, and bustling. A wall of wine bottles decorates the bar. Outside seating is available on East 4th Street. The cuisine is presented in rustic style (no frou frou plating here) and has, of course, won awards, with Symon being recognized with the 2009 James Beard Foundation Award for Best Chef Great Lakes Region.

"I cook the food and flavors that I was raised with. It is definitely driven by meat but also inspired by my heritage and the Eastern European flavors of Cleveland."
–Michael Symon

Left: A favorite on the Lola menu is braised beef cheek pierogi, Symon's homage to the city's Eastern European culinary roots.

Middle: Lola is an anchor eatery on E. 4th Street

Right: Symon shares his cooking skills in his restaurants, in cookbooks and on TV. (Photos courtesy of Michael Symon Restaurants)

Meat is unabashedly the specialty, though there are also some vegetarian and seafood options, including Dover sole. Symon's signature dish has been and continues to be an appetizer of braised beef cheek pierogi with wild mushrooms and horseradish crème frâiche. It's melt-in-your-mouth decadence. Lola's charcuterie plate is also eye-popping. Continue your meal with a smoked pork chop, a great hangar steak, or the lamb shank, made with olives and served with couscous in tribute to his Greek heritage. A side of sea salt and rosemary fries is a must-do. Save room for the cheese board featuring local creations or the brioche French toast with maple bacon ice cream and caramelized apples.

A staff sommelier leads guests through the expensive wine list, which you may peruse, along with beer, cocktails, and other libations on an iPad.

The Symon empire has expanded to B Spot hamburger joints in the suburbs, Mabel's BBQ on 4th Street (see page 18), and other spots out of town. These days Symon broadcasts and spends much of his time in New York City. When he is in town, you may catch him at a culinary show, fundraiser, or book signing. He's the author of several best-selling cookbooks, including *Carnivore: 120 Recipes for Meat Lovers* (2012) and the new *Playing With Fire* (2018). He and his wife, Liz, also operate a B&B, SymonHouse, in the historic Tremont neighborhood (available for rent via Airbnb).

2058 E. 4th St.
216-621-5652
lolabistro.com

BUTCHER AND THE BREWER

A beer hall on East 4th, the restaurant street

Downtown, on the bustling E. 4th Street pedestrian walkway that leads to some of the city's best restaurants, the Butcher and the Brewer is an ambitious operation that combines a popular German-style beer hall in a one-hundred-year-old warehouse and meals that are served European style, as they are ready from the kitchen. Diners eat at long tables that are considered communal and inviting for meeting and mixing. Management says its mission "encourages interaction and a sense of community through public house seating, progressive dining, and shared plates."

The kitchen, with an in-house butcher and charcutier, supports local farmers. The brewery is also in-house (head downstairs to see the tanks). The "cured" list features house-made charcuterie selections. "Cultured" covers local cheese and meats, including steak tartare made with beer mustard. The raw oysters and beer form a delightful culinary marriage.

A butcher shop, off the street, sells take-home, such as chicken, house-made sausages, and smoked lamb ribs along with other Cleveland-made foodstuffs. You can also pick up sandwiches featuring house corned beef, house smoked turkey, and the like.

2043 E. 4th St.
216-331-0805
butcherandthebrewer.com

Top: A lunchtime crowd fills the tables along busy E. 4th Street

Bottom: You can do takeout from the market where house-cured meats, choice cuts, and prepared foods are featured.

MABEL'S BBQ

The trendiest BBQ joint in town

Mabel's showcases what celebrity chef Michael Symon can do with pork and brisket and Flintstones-sized beef ribs. It's on East 4th Street near the much fancier Lola (see page 14). Ribs are Ohio pork, and the BBQ sauce features local Bertman Original Ball Park Mustard (see page 202).

The voluminous two-level restaurant is done up in roadhouse rustic, complete with piles of real wood (used in the smoking process). A long bar runs down one side, and while there are individual tables, the fun here comes getting sloppy at the communal tables. The portions are huge and served on butcher paper–covered trays. The meat is accompanied by an expansive bourbon list, including private barrel selections. Among the couple of dozen beers on draught is one featuring Symon's own recipe.

You can impress your friends by ordering sides of pig parts, such as tails, ears, and cracklins, but the calling card is the ribs, which Larry Olmstead of *USA Today* raved are "among the best ribs you can eat in America." That said, Mabel's isn't a perfect choice for vegetarians. The red neon sign flashing in the window says "EAT MORE MEAT," and even the greens (kale and collard) are cooked with bacon.

There is a locavore element at play at Mabel's. In addition to Ohio pork and local mustard, the bread comes from the West Side Market, the sauerkraut is Cleveland Kraut brand, and the pickles are Cleveland Pickle.

Top left: Eating on the pedestrian mall of E. 4th Street. (Photo by David G. Molyneaux)

Top right: Order "This Is Cleveland" and you will get kielbasa, spare ribs, pork roll, and cabbage. (Photo courtesy of Michael Symon's Restaurants)

Above left: It is all about the meat at Michael Symon's BBQ joint. (Photo courtesy of Michael Symon's Restaurants)

Above right: Creative sides include spaetzle and cabbage, cole slaw with poppy seed, cucumber sour cream salad, crispy potatoes with bacon vinaigrette (Photo courtesy of Michael Symon's Restaurants)

2050 E. 4th St.
216-417-8823
mabelsbbq.com

Wonder how Michael Symon came up with the names for his Cleveland restaurants? Lola (see page 14) is his aunt. Mabel is his dog, a bullmastiff.

BLUE POINT GRILLE

Shucking 75,000 oysters each year

For twenty years, the Blue Point has been one of the city's top downtown seafood choices, especially for a date night. Its grand and classy multilevel fine-dining room commands the corner position in a restored property in the historic Warehouse District. The Hoyt Building, constructed in 1875, is representative of a style that followed the development of cast iron. The building has cast-iron posts on the ground floor facades and masonry walls. It was used for offices and retail businesses.

Today, towering dining room windows overlook the heart of downtown. The ceiling is high, with chandeliers. Columns are topped in gold, and tables are set with linen. Diners enjoy Alaskan King Crab, chilled seafood towers, lobster bisque, Maine Gulf salmon, and day boat cod, and Certified Angus Beef steaks are on the menu too. The restaurant shucks more than seventy-five thousand fresh oysters each year for the raw bar. The wine list, with choices by the glass, is extensive.

The Blue Point Grille is a popular stop on late weekday afternoons at one of the city's best happy hours, when the primary lure is Blue Point oysters from Long Island Sound at two dollars each, served in the bar, where libations play second fiddle. Shrimp and crab claws are four for eight dollars. Try the ceviche with jalapeño, lime, cilantro, and red onion. The bar is friendly, the dress code elegant casual.

700 W. St. Clair Ave.
216-875-7827
bluepointgrille.com

Blue Point's dining room at W. 6th Street and St. Clair Avenue points toward Public Square downtown.

JOHNNY'S DOWNTOWN

Refined dining with a stylish crowd, nightly piano

On the summer evenings when Mike Petrone parks his Band on a Flatbed Truck to play outdoors at West 6th and Frankfurt in the Warehouse District, Johnny's Downtown feels like the center of the city. Glasses clink at tables packed with romance and laughter under an awning along the front of one of Cleveland's classic fine-dining restaurants. As the band plays, dancing high heels click on the sidewalk.

Year-round, Johnny's Downtown draws a stylish business and social crowd, as it has since 1993. That's when owner Joe Santosuosso borrowed the substance of his near West Side restaurant, Johnny's Bar on Fulton Road, lowered the lights, and bumped up the atmosphere a few notches to open one of the city's more sophisticated establishments. Like the restaurant, pianist and singer Petrone is a Cleveland tradition, performing in the bar weeknights 6:00–10:00. (Cliff Habian plays on Saturdays.)

Santosuosso, who is always on the lookout for celebrities in town, was smart to bring much of the Fulton Road menu to the refurbished 1860s downtown building, formerly a general store. The kitchen focuses on rich flavors and textures of upscale Italian fare—pasta, veal, and fish—as well as steaks. Try the mussels Provençal; sautéed frog legs; steamed littleneck clams with andouille, chick peas, blistered tomatoes, fennel, and garlic crostini; potato-crusted grouper; and angel hair pasta with veal meatballs and great-grandmother's marinara sauce (also sold in bottles to take home).

In the same building around the corner on Frankfurt Avenue is Santosuosso's smallest Johnny, called the Little Bar because of its size. The tavern is cozy and casual, a come-as-you-are kind of place with old wood tables, exposed brick walls, neon signs, a jukebox, and

Top left: The sidewalk on W. 6th Street rocks on summer nights when the Band on a Flatbed Truck is in town.

Right: A busy summer night on Johnny's W. 6th Street patio.

Above left: Inside, Johnny's has a sophisticated, special-occasion feel.

posters from the past—JFK is running for president. Occasionally, the quiet hideaway lures a celebrity passing through town. One night George Clooney stopped by to drink, dance, and sing.

Patrons at Johnny's Little Bar celebrate the award-winning burger, made from the steak carvings at Johnny's Downtown and packed loosely, served with house-made chips. The tavern is open daily until 2:30 a.m., serving several dozen choices of beers, Italian dishes, and a late-night menu.

Johnny's Downtown
1406 W. 6th St.
216-623-0055
johnnyscleveland.com

Johnny's Little Bar
614 Frankfort Ave.
216-861-2166

HEINEN'S GROCERY STORE DOWNTOWN CLEVELAND

Downtown treasure in a classic rotunda

Stop by for the food either in prepared form or groceries to cook your own meal. Take an extra few minutes to admire the architecture at this downtown grocery store on the corner of East 9th Street and Euclid Avenue. The store occupies the rotunda of an iconic city building built for the Cleveland Trust bank in 1908 when the city was in its early-twentieth-century golden age as one of the top 10 cities in the country. The New York designer was renowned George B. Post, an architect trained in the Beaux-Arts tradition. Murals were painted by artist Francis Millet, who later perished in the Titanic disaster.

Head upstairs for a "secret" imbibing spot with self-serve wine, local craft beers, and snacks. Under the dome of stained glass, you can nibble chef-prepared dishes, such as wraps, salads, and rice bowls.

Once refreshed, peruse the shelves downstairs for local products, such as Chef Zack Bruell's sauces and olive oil, Johnny's Marinara, locally grown products from area farms, Heinen's-labled products, and prepared foods. With origins in 1929 and locations in the suburbs, too, Heinen's is Cleveland's oldest family-owned grocer, akin to a Whole Foods, only better.

900 Euclid Ave.
216-302-3020
heinens.com

Left: Expect to be wowed by both the architecture and food selections at Heinen's downtown, in a landmark old bank building.

Right: Head upstairs from the grocery selection to see what local and other Midwestern regional craft beers are on tap, for sipping and light eating. The menu changes weekly. Brews are available by the glass, half growler, and growler.

MALLORCA

Dressed the way fine dining used to look

Mallorca, downtown a few blocks from Public Square, takes you back a couple of decades, and that is all good, from the quaint room to the fine dining, old style. Even the patio is dressed formally, with white linen tablecloths. Inside and out, cloth napkins are carefully folded. Waiters in tuxedoes provide fine-tuned service. Menus are leatherbound. The wine list has selections from around the world, hundreds of them, as recognized by *Wine Spectator* magazine.

Seafood is a specialty. Real paella is the big attraction, Valencia-style, filled with shrimp, scallops, clams, mussels, and a half-lobster as well as chicken and sausage and served in a traditional two-handled paella pan. Mallorca's chef is Spanish, and the restaurant offers the best Spanish and Portuguese cuisine in town. Featured Portuguese dishes are *sopa de ajo* (garlic soup) and shrimp in garlic sauce (as an appetizer or entrée). Appetizers include mushrooms stuffed with crab meat and mascarpone. For entrées, consider lobster tails, Madrid-style veal scallopini with roast peppers in a lemon wine sauce, and broiled pork chops with garlic sauce.

Portions are big. Entrées come with saffron rice, Spanish potatoes, and vegetables. Throughout the dining room, you can smell the wonderful saffron. Ask for house-made sangria. Occasionally, the restaurant will have special wine events as listed on their website.

1390 W. 9th St.
216-687-9494
clevelandmallorca.com

Top left: The main dining of Mallorca, dressed and ready for dinner.

Top right: Mallorca's entrance has a classic and playful look.

Above left: Dark wood defines the bar at Mallorca

Above right: A couple dines at lunch in a quiet corner of Mallorca's side dining room.

MARBLE ROOM

Steaks, raw bar where millions of dollars once changed hands

The first impression walking in off the street in the heart of downtown is that the Marble Room is spectacular—grand, shining, and stunning, an architectural marvel. You look around the cavernous old bank building lobby and know instinctively that a significant portion of the former bank's profits never left this room. The Marble Room is a wow, and you hope that dinner is nearly as good.

A restaurant designer said that the name Marble Room refers both to the dominant material in the banking hall and to the idea that a juicy steak should be nicely marbled. Top steaks plus a big raw bar are featured on the menu of this fine-dining establishment opened in 2017. It's expensive—the priciest restaurant in the city—but that has not stopped the flow of customers who come for drinks, pre-theater suppers, full multicourse dinners, and—consistently a winner—the opportunity to ogle the room.

Fluted Corinthian columns in pink Georgia marble rise thirty-five feet, towering over a thirty-three-foot-long bar, dining tables, and banquettes with a total of 225 seats. Many of the original bank design elements have been repurposed. The legs of check-cashing stations now support bar tables. Nearly a thousand safety deposit boxes left behind have been incorporated into the Marble Room design, as in the front of the lower-level bar.

If you plan dinner at a table, make a reservation. Steaks start at a petit filet and go up to a forty-ounce porterhouse and a forty-two-ounce long-bone tomahawk. You'll find the usual sides, including creamed spinach and truffle *pomme frites*. Without reservations, your best shot at a long look at one of the most photographed restaurants you will ever see is to look for a spot at the long bar. Have a drink and

Left: The Marble Room captures imaginations and wonder.
Right: Dining in the bank vault of the Marble Room. (Photos courtesy of the Marble Room)

order from a menu that includes items from the raw seafood bar and such small plates as a fish-n-chips sushi roll and beef tartare (made with prime tenderloin) served with house-made bagel chips.

A plaque hangs on Euclid Avenue outside the Marble Room, reminding diners that National City Bank, a city landmark, had been in business since 1845. The elegant lobby was renovated in 1915 by Cleveland's famed architectural firm Walker and Weeks and was reported to be an interpretation of the neoclassical Beaux-Arts style. Ninety-three years later the bank was sold during the subprime mortgage market failures of 2008. A few blocks away and across the street is another reminder of a once-proud, dominant local and regional bank. The Cleveland Trust Rotunda has been architecturally repurposed as the world's most beautiful grocery store, Heinen's (see page 24), which serves the growing downtown population.

623 Euclid Ave.
216-523-7000
marbleroomcle.com

PURA VIDA BY BRANDT

Comfort food with vegan options in a nightclub-like downtown setting

Chef Brandt Evans opened this downtown restaurant near Tower City keeping in mind that not every office worker wants meat. His creative American menu offers a choice, for instance— go full-on vegan with the African peanut stew or pig out on Korean fried chicken.

Evans trained at the Culinary Institute of America and worked for Charlie Palmer in Manhattan. He has creds. His restaurant occupies the first floor of the old May Department Stores Company building. The décor is urban swanky in a 1990s kind of way, with white, cloudlike drapes across the ceiling and colored mood lights. Views through tall windows are right onto Public Square. Sit in the patio and you'll be among downtown's high-rises as you sip craft beverages.

Brandt creatively uses fresh, sustainable ingredients in such dishes as a vegan Caesar, vegan chopped salad, vegan nachos, or the playful chick pea jar or Veggie Mac served in a box—dishes that won him acclaim from the *HappyCow* vegan blog. Meat eaters can indulge in other menu favorites, including flank steak salad or bacon-wrapped pork tenderloin. Brandt smartly has something to please everyone in your party.

The first Tuesday of every month is vegan club, featuring social vegan happy hours, wine tasting, and cooking classes (reservations required).

Left: The restaurant's decor and lighting are retro cool.. Diners feel as if they are in a hip nightlife spot.

Right: Those who do not eat animal products will not feel deprived with such a dish as chicken-fried cauliflower with vegan white pepper gravy. (Photos courtesy of pura_vida_by_brandt via Instagram)

170 Euclid Ave.
216-987-0100
puravidabybrandt.com

NAUTI MERMAID

Key West island attitude near Lake Erie shore

A crab shack awaits in the Warehouse District just a few blocks from the freshwater Lake Erie shore, which is at least several hundred miles from the nearest ocean and more than 1,200 miles from Key West. But the neon blue mermaid that hangs outside and a kitschy interior, including lobster traps and floatation devices, wood tables, and a neon Live Bait sign, flash a message about hanging around the Florida Keys. Key West photos are on the walls.

The casual, Caribbean-inspired long bar and restaurant serves lobster and crab sandwiches as well as heavily breaded and fried items ranging from crab cakes and conch fritters to spicy fish and vegetarian tacos as well as burgers and jerk chicken, all prepared with Caribbean spices. Key lime pie is well worth an order.

Lunch has a popular eight-dollar menu that includes peel-and-eat shrimp, sliders, fish and chips, or a half-dozen oysters. Happy hour Wednesdays are led by one-dollar oysters. Try the lobster soup with jalapeño cream. The bar is lively, with beer on tap and frequently hums with live music (schedule available on the website). Open until 2:30 a.m. Jeffrey Hassan, the owner, is a Cleveland State University alum.

1378 W. 6th St.
216-771-6175
thenautimermaid.com

Left: Cleveland's Nauti Mermaid has a Key West, Florida vibe.

Above: Oysters and a terrific key lime pie highlight the menu.

SLYMAN'S

Where laborers, suits, and a President eat corned beef

For more than half a century, an eatery has stood on St. Clair Avenue near East 31st Street. First, it was Larry's Jewish deli, owned by the late Lawrence Leuchtag. Since 1964, it has been Slyman's, which was opened by Rafic Abdallah Slyman, who emigrated from Lebanon and bought the business with the goal of feeding his seven brothers and sisters. Abdallah's family, which is Christian, decided to use their last name on the restaurant when they moved into what was a Jewish neighborhood. Joseph Slyman, Rafic's brother, and his wife, Mae, worked the deli as a family business for decades until their son Freddie took over. Freddie Slyman, now fifty-one and owner with his brother Moe, manned the slicer starting at age nineteen.

Keys to success are the friendly, personal atmosphere and monster-sized sandwiches, led by their famous behemoth corned beef sandwich ($15) that holds twelve to fourteen ounces of beef, cooked daily starting at 3:00 a.m. Big sandwiches are also stuffed with roast beef, pastrami, turkey, or ham. "My dad's big hands made the big

---

"Waiter: someone ate the other half of my sandwich"

Slyman's sells the best corned beef in Cleveland. Don't be dissuaded by naysayers who insist that one person cannot consume an entire monster-sized sandwich at lunch. The sandwich is served cut in half, and while the first half is satisfying, you might just nibble on the second half, which you had considered saving as possibly a meal for dinner. Soon, it has also vanished. With that for lunch, more often than not, you will not hunger for dinner.

Left: Slyman has been working the corned beef slicer since he was nineteen years old.

Right: Slyman's sign is small, but the line of customers can curl out the front door and onto St. Clair Avenue.

sandwiches," says Freddie. "He always said, 'This will keep the people coming back.'"

Until expansion into a dining room in 1988, the deli was a "hole in the wall," says Freddie, with just two counters and five tables. "Slyman's was built on regulars," he says. "We used to know everyone by name. Now it's become a bit of a tourist attraction. We've been referred to as an 'institution,' and we're honored to have that reputation."

President George W. Bush stopped by in 2007 for a corned beef sandwich, eating while secret service agents frisked fellow customers waiting in line to get in the door for lunch. "He comes in, and he does his president thing," Freddie says. "We got some pictures, I gave him a T-shirt, and bid him adieu."

The deli has not changed its recipes or suppliers since 1964. Orlando Baking Co. and Vienna Distributing Co., both Cleveland businesses, supply the bread and meat. The family has opened Slyman's Taverns in the suburbs, while a cousin, Samir Elnehas, who emigrated from Lebanon at the age of eighteen, works in the deli downtown.

3106 St. Clair Ave.
216-621-3760

The downtown food truck scene

A sure sign that spring is arriving is the emergence of about twenty food trucks surrounding a one-acre square, originally a sunken design by I. M. Pei, but made decisively brighter and cheerier in a $3 million renovation in 2011 of Perk Plaza at Chester Commons.

Under bright red trellises and some greenery, downtown workers and others lured by the event sit at picnic tables or on the concrete steps and dive into such treats as award-winning, slow-cooked barbecue pork or brisket or bacon on a stick from The Proper Pig, BettysBombAssBurgers, and the gooiest, tastiest, I-can't-believe-it's-not-meat vegan "meatball" sub from Wild Spork (the secret is in the cashew "cheese," the texture of the "meat," and the delicious marinara sauce).

New trucks appear each year. In 2018, an addition was Executive Grill, a food bus operated by city high school culinary students. Creativity abounds. For instance, SWAT, out of Macedonia, Ohio, has on its menu tater tots topped with crab and lobster Rangoon and crunchy onions. It's extremely decadent!

The feasting occurs Wednesdays, May through September, from 11:00 a.m. to 1:30 p.m. Arrive early or late to avoid long lines. The gathering, which also sometimes includes live music, is sponsored by the nonprofit Downtown Cleveland Alliance.

Chester Commons, East 12th Street and Chester Avenue
216-736-7799 (Downtown Cleveland Alliance)
downtowncleveland.com/events/walnut-wednesday

Top left: Wild Spork, out of Lake County to the East, serves vegan cuisine. The menu includes an insane "meatball" sub.

Top right: Forget about the calories and indulge in tater tots topped with crab and lobster Rangoon, from SWAT.

Above left: Fired Up Taco Truck specializes in bold flavors with a menu of creative tacos, empanadas, and seasoned battered fries.

Above right: Taste of Nawln's serves up Low Country New Orleans dishes such as a rich chicken and andouille gumbo.

For additional outdoor fun, TGIFTF (Thank Goodness It's Food Truck Friday!) events take place on Fridays, May to October in Willard Park in front of the FREE stamp sculpture and City Hall (at the corner of E. 9th and Lakeside Ave.), 11:00 a.m. to 1:30 p.m. Usually, nine or so trucks arrive each week along with local entertainers. The gathering is sponsored by the City of Cleveland. facebook.com/FTFCleveland/

PROSPERITY SOCIAL CLUB

Tremont dive from the 1930s with a retro vibe today

A lot of yesterday hangs in the air at Tremont's Prosperity Social Club—on its walls and in the life reflected in the long, mirrored bar. In rooms that look like someplace your grandparents might have hung out—or at least grandpa—Prosperity is not a club, nor merely a restaurant or tavern. It is a social gathering place where at least four generations of blue-collar local patrons (and more recently hipsters) have been eating and drinking, hoping that prosperity was just around the corner. The décor is as old as the bar itself, which doesn't account for the years that the early owner sold Prohibition-era bootleg whiskey just two doors away.

Nearly everyone seems to know everybody else inside this neighborhood icon, but strangers are welcomed with smiles and conversation, as they have been since Tremont's workers stopped here on their walk home from the steel mills and factories down the hill in Cleveland's industrial flats. With a beer in a fish bowl and sometimes a boilermaker (beer with a shot of whiskey) or two, downtime at the "club" helped the transition from heavy work to a small, simple home.

Descriptions of the past come from the family of Stan Dembowski, who bought the building called Hot Dog Bills and began selling hot dogs out of the front window in 1938. Dembowski opened the tavern inside as Dempsey's Night Club, changing the name to Dempsey's Oasis to draw a bigger, less dressy crowd. His wife cooked and cleaned. He built up the business by cashing payroll checks and serving sixteen-oz. fish bowls of beer with various liquors at a cheap price. His first food was salty pretzels and cheese corn, which he placed on the bar and at tables so that the guys would stick around and have another boilermaker. Many a man would crack a raw egg into his fish bowl for five cents more, supposedly to put a little more "lead in their pencil."

Top left: Prosperity is a rollicking, friendly place to eat and drink.

Above left: Prosperity kitchen turns out some of the best pierogies in town. They come stuffed with either mashed potatoes and cheese or dry ricotta. Both are pan-fried and served with sautéed onions and sour cream.

Right: From a front window, Hot Dog Bills dispensed sandwiches in 1938.

After World War II came fish fries and homemade pierogis on Fridays and then live entertainment (polka bands, musical shows, and comedians) on weekends, when they played on a small stage in the backroom.

Today, patrons stop in the vintage games room for pinball, the old-fashioned bowling machine, and tavern food that won't clean out your wallet, open daily until midnight. On Sundays, Prosperity is a fried chicken dinner (three pieces) at eleven dollars, served with Southern greens and homemade mac & cheese. Add a liter of sangria for fourteen dollars. Monday is wing dang doodle, tasty chicken wings (including a vegan "wing" basket), draft beer, and a curated playlist of vintage electric blues and classic R&B. Pierogis stuffed with potatoes and cheese or dry ricotta are available every night.

1109 Starkweather Ave.
216-937-1938
prosperitysocialclub.com

Asian fusion and intimacy in Tremont

A Tremont neighborhood anchor eatery, Parallax is the flagship restaurant of owner Zack Bruell, who puts his personal chef stamp on nearly every item, from the taste of the rice in sushi to the popular entrée Peking chicken (not duck).

The setting at Parallax is intimate and sophisticated, the menu a fascinating collection of choices from pork shank pad Thai, tempura tofu, and Korean braised beef to sesame crusted salmon, red curry cobia, miso-glazed Alaskan black cod, sushi, sashimi, and hand rolls. Sushi is half price in the bar each Friday and Saturday night after 10:00.

Bruell, who has been nominated for James Beard awards, has been introducing Clevelanders to his take on the West Coast's style of bistro and Asian fusion cuisine since the early 1980s. In 2004, he opened Parallax (derived from an ancient Greek word, it means alternation, its appearance changing as viewed from different angles). Fourteen years later, his restaurant collection, each different in style and menu, has grown to nine eateries, all within the city limits—as shopping centers and other commercial developments have been unsuccessful in their attempts to tempt him to the suburbs.

"Dining is about escape," says Bruell. "My restaurants are about an escape to somewhere else—Parallax to SoHo, Alley Cat Oyster Bar to the waters in Santa Barbara, L'Albatros to a neighborhood in Paris. Collision Bend Brewing Company is quintessential Cleveland on the Cuyahoga River. Each has a different menu. We

> "I will be a success when I am playing golf every day."
> –Zack Bruell, owner of nine eateries in Cleveland

Top left: Sushi and sashimi, including a variety of rolls, are among specialties at Parallax, an Asian fusion restaurant.

Top right: Parallax fits well into the neighborhood of restored buildings in Tremont.

Above left: The dining room at Parallax.

Above right: Prolific Cleveland Chef Zack Bruell. (Photos courtesy of Zack Bruell Restaurant Group).

stayed away from opening restaurants that were only for special occasions or for the expense account crowd. Each menu has items that meet an affordable price point. I want the corporation business, but I don't build a restaurant around that."

Other Bruell eateries include Table 45 at the InterContinental Cleveland, Chinato, Cowell & Hubbard, DYNOMITE hamburgers at Playhouse Square, and Exploration at the Cleveland Museum of Natural History. Bruell also has a line of products at ZackBruell.com, including sauces from his restaurants, olive oil and vinegars, and six blends of coffee.

2179 W. 11th St.
216-583-9999
parallaxtremont.com

FAHRENHEIT

Contemporary regional menu from a gregarious chef

Menu choices change frequently at this Tremont anchor restaurant as Chef Rocco Whalen's creative juices flow. Dinner can be an exploration of taste, for example, classic American with an Asian twist, such as Kobe beef short ribs served on lo-mein noodles. Cleveland nachos come with crispy potato, parmesan fondue, Romano, scallions, and bacon. The kitchen focuses on fresh, seasonal ingredients, many from local and regional farms.

Fahrenheit has a patio out front. Inside, where the rooms once were darker and looked more like a bar, there's a new, stylish décor. Sometimes the restaurant seems like a fancy spot—it is a good choice for special occasions—but Fahrenheit has also maintained that gathering spot feeling, and the bar scene remains fun and chatty through dinner.

Whalen, who paid his early dues working with Wolfgang Puck on the West Coast, opened Fahrenheit in 2002 at the age of twenty-four. He grew up in Charlotte, North Carolina, where he opened a second Fahrenheit location in 2013. Today, he is a devoted Clevelander and a boisterous fan of the professional football team the Cleveland Browns. "I'll be at every Browns game. Count on it," he once told an interviewer.

Gregarious, full of innovative ideas, and willing to experiment, Whalen lost 124 pounds while appearing on the Food Network reality series *Fat Chef*. Today, you can ask for "healthy" "Fahren-lite® Style" items, lower in calories and fat. There is a separate vegan menu. You may go with Rocco's black truffle meatballs, pizza fired in a stone oven and topped with, say, duck confit, and a twenty-two-ounce Ohio pork shank. Or stick with the lower-calorie chicken

Left: The Rocco's brand, which began in Tremont at Fahrenheit, now also shines where the Browns and Cavs play.

Right: Fahrenheit's dining room in Tremont has a new, stylish feel.

breast served with quinoa salad. Vegan options might include a "risotto" made with quinoa, roasted brussels sprouts, candied butternut squash, and pomegranate molasses. The wine list is good but pricey.

If you dine at Fahrenheit, ask for Whalen to stop by the table. The guy loves food, and his patter is infectious.

Chef Whelan has taken his Rocco's brand to his beloved sports scenes and a casino, with a booth at the Q (Quicken Loans Arena) where the Cleveland Cavaliers play, another at FirstEnergy Stadium that is home to the Browns, and the casual Rosie and Rocco's restaurant at the JACK Cleveland Casino. Fahrenheit's food truck was chosen as one of the "Best Food Trucks in the Nation" in 2011 by *Antenna* magazine.

2417 Professor Ave.
216-781-8858
chefroccowhalen.com/fahrenheit-cleveland

Funky hangout in Tremont since the '90s

The best reason to seek a meal in the Tremont neighborhood just south of downtown is the breadth and depth of intriguing eateries. A table always seems to be available somewhere, with a chef who will reward your choice, such as at the funky gastropub in the one-hundred-year-old house and outdoor patio known as Fat Cats.

While local chef and TV star Michael Symon rightfully gets credit for starting the Tremont culinary revolution in the late 1990s, other entrepreneurial food pioneers also braved the opportunity to move into a faded neighborhood and start cooking and experimenting with tastes and styles that were new to Cleveland. Ricardo Sandoval was one of the trailblazers, opening Fat Cats in 1997, within months of Symon's opening of famed Lola.

"I chose to be part of the renaissance of Tremont," says Sandoval. "I love the balance of people from various socioeconomic backgrounds. They include generations of families, artists, and young professionals. The proximity of Tremont to downtown and to history makes it the crown jewel neighborhood of Cleveland."

Sandoval owns an urban garden on a valuable piece of land near Fat Cats that he says will always stay green as well as an herb garden behind the restaurant and a list of properties he has bought over time using land contracts. He says his goal is to keep the rents low to support growing businesses. "It's my self-imposed style of rent control on Tremont properties," says Sandoval.

Fats Cats, open Monday through Saturday on the north end of Tremont, is a cozy hangout. The patio is pet friendly and serves them a choice of chicken or beef snacks. The menu for humans is a global collection of small and large plates, with a Filipino fusion that originates from Sandoval's family, which arrived in Cleveland in the 1970s. It is vegan friendly.

Left: A well-fed feline look keeps its eyes on the bar at Fats Cats.

Right: Tremont is an old working-class neighborhood where many of its homes have been turned into restaurants, among them Fat Cats in this 100-year-old house.

Come early for a seat at Saturday brunch. Lunches Monday–Friday include a chopped BLT with applewood bacon, kale, slow-roasted cherry tomato, and avocado aioli. Weekday happy hour has an extensive cheap eats menu, including such dishes as butternut squash soup, flavored with turmeric and ginger; banh bao, a sandwich with two steamed buns filled with pork belly or tofu and dressed with pickled daikon, hoisin, jalapeño, and cilantro; seasonal risotto; sweet potato fried shrimp with sweet and sour dipping sauce; and a pork belly salad with vermicelli noodles, veggies, and a chili dressing. The Fat Monday dinner special is three courses for twenty-five dollars from a menu that includes such items through the week as steamed clams with red curry, ginger, garlic and cilantro; grilled octopus with onion, avocado, shaved cauliflower, lemon and olive oil; and beef lumpia with bavette beef, cabbage, pickled carrots, and spicy house mustard.

Don't hurry in or out of Fats Cats. Inside and outdoors are great views of downtown, which was built on a bluff just to the north across the valley of the wiggling Cuyahoga River.

2061 W. 10th St.
216-579-0200
facebook.com/FatsCatsCleveland

DANTE

Pairing a chef's food and love of rock 'n' roll

The building complex in the Tremont neighborhood that houses Dante Boccuzzi's culinary playground is more than a single eatery. Four establishments call 2247 Professor Avenue home, and you could make a day of tasting Dante's concoctions. Start with brunch or a lunch at the casual trattoria that Boccuzzi calls Dante Next Door, which sits next door to the main restaurant, Dante. After shopping and exploring Tremont, you might do a kind of a progressive dinner, first with happy hour sushi at Ginko (see page 48), downstairs from Dante, followed by dinner—Mediterranean-tinged, Asian-inspired, new American style—at at Dante itself, perhaps sitting at a table in the old vault of the bank building where Dante is located. Diners may choose from small plates of pasta or risotto; big plates, such as linguini alla carbonara; or a multicourse chef's menu. (You also could skip the first course at Boccuzzi's sushi place and order some of Ginko's specialties as an appetizer at Dante).

Still feeling progressive? Check out the music, especially at Thursday's singer/songwriter nights, beneath Dante Next Door at cozy and artsy Coda. In music, the coda is the concluding passage of a piece or movement, typically forming an addition to the basic structure. Coda, underground with brick and colorful murals, fits well the lifestyle of chef Dante Boccuzzi, who is also a rock and blues guitarist and singer known for pairing food with rock 'n' roll. Hungry? Coda has a simple evening menu, or you could head back upstairs to Dante for late-night noodles.

Boccuzzi, a native Clevelander, has been recognized nationally with two James Beard Foundation Rising Star nominations. His main culinary mentor was celebrity chef Charlie Palmer, who encouraged him to travel abroad for more experience. Great food like great

Top: Chef Dante Boccuzzi is a guitarist and signer who pairs food with rock 'n' roll.
Above left: The menu satisfies cravings for new American, Asian and Mediterranean flavors.
Above right: Dinner at Dante in the old bank vault. (Photos courtesy of Dante)

music depends on a mix of technique and heart, says Boccuzzi, who has chopped and played music around the globe as he worked in kitchens in Italy, France, England, China, and Taiwan.

On a busy night, Dante, which opened in 2007, can get noisy, but it is a grand place and frequently does wine dinners. After dinner, grab a handful of candy at the door—classic stuff, such as Tootsie Rolls and fireballs. If you are in Cleveland for a baseball game at Progressive Field, Dante has a food booth called, of course, Inferno.

2247 Professor Ave.
216-274-1200
danteboccuzzi.com

Real sushi in the Rust Belt

In a tiny basement in Tremont, good things happen with sushi. Come here for the level of preparation you'd expect to find on the East or West Coast. Owner Dante Boccuzzi (whose namesake restaurant is located upstairs) did some training in Japan and knows traditional Japanese cuisine. He has fresh fish flown in from the Tsukiji Fish Market in Tokyo and leaves the careful manipulation to his Japanese chef.

The menu naturally focuses heavily on raw fish accompanied by a good selection of sakes, Japanese beer, and specialty cocktails. You can order a la carte or do a complete omakase (chef's choice) tasting at prices some Clevelanders might find steep.

For those who don't do raw, vegan options are available, or you can go with cook-your-own Certified Angus Beef shabu-shabu (available at tables only). Start your meal with edamame or blistered shishito peppers, or experience Dante's creativity in three styles of raw oysters or truffled lobster miso soup. The shiny red and black lacquer décor makes this a nice date spot even if you cuddle up in corner stools at the sushi bar.

2247 Professor Ave.
216-274-1202
restaurantginko.com

Left: Grab a booth or watch the expert sushi chefs do their thing from your seat at the counter.

Top right: Raw selections at Ginko are a feast for the eyes and palate.

Above right: The interior is hip and romantic. (Photos courtesy of Dante)

LUCKY'S CAFE

Bakery enriches breakfast, lunch, takeout

Waffles are gingerbread topped with warm maple-roasted apples. The signature biscuits and gravy—TV chef Michael Symon loved this item on the Food Network show *The Best Thing I Ever Ate*—is a collection of cheddar scallion buttermilk biscuits, soft scrambled eggs, and sausage gravy, plus flavorful fried potatoes (and grapes to lighten things up). Corned beef is brined for a week. Mac-n-cheese is made of cheddar, Brie, Parmesan, and mozzarella, baked with cream, and topped with brioche bread crumbs. To any order, you may add a side dish of bacon, cooked with brown sugar and pecans on top.

The rich menu is enticing, but you don't have to eat heavy at breakfast or lunch at the Tremont neighborhood café. Lucky's owner and head chef Heather Haviland loads the house-made granola with rolled oats, spelt, wheat germ, and flax seeds. Smoothies are mixed with local yogurt. Try the broccoli soup or the curried chicken salad sandwich served on house-made multigrain bread with lettuce, pickle, and potato salad. She sources her seasonal menu of fresh ingredients from suppliers within a one-hundred-mile radius.

Lucky's smartly combines hip eatery and bakery. Behind the brick façade out front is a warm welcoming décor, with tree art on the walls and a glass bakery case from which you may choose something to take home, such as granola or a bag of biscotti.

Expect a crowd for weekend brunches. In good weather, tables are available in the garden outside. When the patio is closed for the season, the café's tight quarters fill up fast. Lucky's main menu is available daily 9:00 a.m. to 3:00 p.m., but if you're early and in a hurry, Monday through Friday you'll find baked goods and a breakfast sandwich available by 7:00 a.m.

Top left: At Lucky's you'll be tempted to bring home a bag of the delicious granola or biscotti, among other treats.

Top right: Diners get an explanation of the restaurant's purpose.

Above left: A patio, open in warm weather, doubles the capacity for Lucky's.

Above right: A mural catches the Tremont history of factory and mill workers, and smokestacks.

777 Starkweather Ave.
216-622-7773
luckyscafe.com

No grumps allowed at this popular breakfast spot

This bright, airy, happy restaurant in the Tremont neighborhood, a ten-minute drive south of downtown, focuses on a big menu for daily breakfasts and other comfort foods during daily lunch and weekend dinners. The slogan is "Cleveland feel good food." You may as well leave your troubles at home because nobody seems to be grumpy at Grumpy's, with the possible exception of first-timers who arrive during the prime hours for Sunday brunch, not knowing about waiting in a line that can flow out the door and down the sidewalk. (The line moves fast but never fast enough, so regulars learn when to time their visit, such as NOT in the thirty to forty-five minutes after local churches conclude their services.) Once inside the Cleveland landmark, smiling waitstaff and happy eaters will chase away any lingering impatience.

Grumpy's is a homey place. Owner Kathy Owad hangs works by local artists on the walls. Food is prepared by hand, as the staff cuts each potato, and bread is baked each morning. Eggs dishes are a specialty, including in skillet, omelet, and Benedict form, served with Cajun home fries. You may also order a big variety of pancakes (even potato or sweet potato pancakes), French toast, waffles, breakfast burritos, and even breakfast tacos with chorizo. The Carminator is scrambled eggs, bacon, spinach, mixed grilled veggies, and Swiss cheese with chipotle mayo wrapped in a whole-wheat tortilla. There's a burger on the menu too.

There is a real Grumpy. When the original owner, Scott Lindell, was renovating a building to house his new restaurant in the city's blue-collar working-class neighborhood, he fell through a staircase, breaking an ankle. He spent the summer of 1994 on crutches,

Top left: Wheat French toast encrusted in walnuts and topped with apples and a cinnamon honey glaze, is well worth the calories. The accompanying Cajun fries is a savory bonus.

Top right: At certain times on Sunday mornings, the brunch line snakes out the door and down the sidewalk.

Above left: Local art hangs in the main dining room.

Above right: Grumpy T's and Grumpy mugs are big sellers.

muttering and complaining his way through the remodeling. His new nickname, Grumpy, stuck.

The restaurant has had its share of adversity and a big rebound. Six months after Owad bought it from Grumpy Lindell, a fire destroyed the building that housed the eatery. With the help of friends and patrons, Owad found a new home nearby and two years later opened with a new design, resembling a coastal bed and breakfast in Maine, and a dining room three times the size of the original, which is why the line outside moves along at a good pace.

2621 W. 14th St.
216-241-5025
grumpys-cafe.com

USHABU

DIY cooking with gourmet flair

Cleveland had no official shabu-shabu restaurant when Matthew Spinner opened this chic little Japanese restaurant a couple of years ago in the Tremont neighborhood. The chef grew up in Northeast Ohio and paid his culinary dues in Europe and around the United States.

For the uninitiated, shabu-shabu is a cook-it-yourself hot pot dish. You pick a broth, which is kept hot on a burner, and cook your choice of thinly sliced protein or vegetables in the simmering liquid. Spinner features local meats, such as Wagyu beef raised in Mount Vernon, Ohio, and smoked local pork belly, as well as market-fresh fish and vegetable options. Broth choices include kombu dashi, ginger chicken, or caramelized miso. Your meal also comes with sides of assorted vegetables, firm tofu, and ramen noodles.

Sitting at the counter while you cook is a great conversation starter. There are tables if you come with friends, and you can accompany your meal with tastings from the extensive sake menu. Spinner also presents an impressive array of creative, albeit pricey, appetizers, or you can splurge on a five-course hikoushiki kaiseki menu with bites that include an A5 wagyu tartar with a Kumamoto oyster and "prestige" caviar.

2173 Professor Ave.
216-713-1741
ushabu.com

Left: Japanese letters on the street sign for Tremont's Ushabu, serving shabu-shabu, a popular hot pot dish in Japan.

Top right: The original artwork on the wall is a compilation of restaurant receipts.

Above right: Reservations are highly recommended as Ushabu is a small restaurant. At peak times, diners are asked to share a booth on one side of the room or sit at the counter.

SOKOLOWSKI'S UNIVERSITY INN

This is the place to *Zjeść obfite* (Polish for "Eat hearty")

One of Cleveland's best-known restaurants opened in 1923 as a tavern with bar food. In the early days, when the Tremont neighborhood was more densely populated with families of the men who worked the nearby mills, Poles rubbed shoulders with Ukrainians, Russians, and a host of other nationalities, all arriving at the inn for tastes of food from their former homes. Life changed in the late 1950s when iron workers on the city's Innerbelt bridge project wanted something more substantial for lunch. Victoria and Michael Sokolowski put together a cafeteria lunch with massive portions of Polish and Eastern European food that remain the primary focus of the menu.

The rustic University Inn is Cleveland's oldest family-owned and -run restaurant, now operated by a third generation of siblings, Mike, Mary, and Bernie Sokolowski. The restaurant is still going strong, serving moderately priced comfort food, just like a Polish grandmother would make. It won a James Beard Award as an American Classic in 2014.

Each weekday and Saturday morning a bell rings in the kitchen at ten minutes before 11:00 for family and staff to gather in front of an image of the Black Madonna. "It's a Polish custom," says a family member. "We owe a lot to Polish pride and prayer." (The Black Madonna of Częstochowa, also known as Our Lady of Częstochowa, is a revered icon of the Virgin Mary at the Jasna Góra Monastery in Częstochowa, Poland.)

As the restaurant family prays, a crowd lines up, awaiting the 11:00 a.m. lunch buffet that typically includes Salisbury steak, bratwurst,

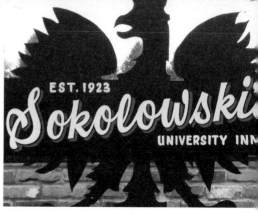

Left: "It's a Kodak moment," said an older gentleman as he walked away from the cafeteria-style line with his stuffed cabbage. "Sometimes a preacher eats well," he said.

Right: Sokolowski's also is called the University Inn because it sits on University Road in the Tremont neighborhood. During the early 1850s, the now defunct Cleveland University briefly occupied a section of Tremont.

kielbasa, sautéed house-made pierogi, chicken paprikash, scrod, and sandwiches, salads, and sides—plenty to sustain the customers if they should decide to go back outside after lunch and build another bridge across the Cuyahoga River valley. Friday lunch also includes a group of fish specials. Sokolowski's serves dinner on Fridays and Saturdays with even larger menus, including such traditional items as Polish stuffed cabbage and rice pudding, familiar to generations of patrons. Live piano music is in the background.

Sokolowski's University Inn is on the northern edge of the Tremont neighborhood overlooking the Cuyahoga River and Cleveland skyline. The walls are filled with hundreds of photos of former visitors, including Jimmy Fallon, Kevin Bacon, David Byrne, and Bill Clinton. Today, the inn is at the spot where the new Cleveland Towpath Extension, part of the Cleveland Metroparks, will briefly exit the old industrial Flats. New green spaces and scenic overlooks are being built. Hungry walkers and bikers wanting a lunch break can join the cafeteria line to experience unique, old-country fare.

1201 University Rd.
216-771-9236
sokolowskis.com

L'ALBATROS

French brasserie shines in University Circle

In an old carriage house on a shaded side street in the middle of the campus of Case Western Reserve University sits a contemporary French brasserie. With a lively dining room and a delicious shaded patio, L'Albatros has a "this is my favorite restaurant" feel. It is among the eclectic city collection of eateries owned by local chef Zack Bruell and is one of the city's prettiest go-to dining spots, especially in summer. In winter, diners find warmth in its intimacy and the glow of a comfy fireplace. But patrons and waiters alike count the days until Northern Ohio finally dives deeply into spring when L'Albatros opens its expansive patio of tables and a bar for the months of warmer nights, with twinkling candlelight under the stars (aided occasionally with outdoor heaters).

Before he opened L'Albatros on the site of a former restaurant (That Place) on University Circle's Bellflower Road, Bruell spent time in Paris researching menus for what he could bring to Cleveland at a reasonably affordable price. His choices ring of France: terrines; a charcuterie platter; escargot; onion soup; chicken liver with fois gras mousseline; mussels with pommes frites; cassoulet of duck confit, lamb, and sausages; bouillabaisse for two; and an extraordinary cheese selection, featuring some of the made-in-Cleveland choices from the Brooklyn Cheese Co.

About the name: L'Albatros is French for albatross, a bird with a huge wingspan that was considered by mariners as good luck as long as the bird was alive. The word "albatross" is sometimes used metaphorically to mean a psychological burden that feels like a curse, an allusion to Samuel Taylor Coleridge's poem "The Rime of the Ancient Mariner" (1798), in which the albatross is hung around a mariner's neck by the crew to symbolize his guilt in killing the bird. Chef Bruell, a top golfer, says he also chose the name from

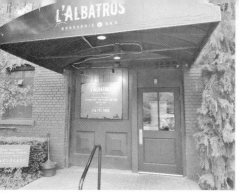

Top left: Entrance to L'Albatros on the campus of Case Western Reserve University.

Top right: As you enter the restaurant, you can catch a glimpse at chef's working in the kitchen.

Above right: L'Albatros patio at University Circle is a favorite dining spot for Clevelanders during warm weather.

Above left: Sophisticated French cuisine is on the menu at L'Albatros. (Photos courtesy of Zack Bruell Restaurant Group)

the British golfing term "albatross," the equivalent of a double eagle, or three under par on a hole—one of golf's most difficult accomplishments.

The restaurant is in a perfect location for a meal on a cultural day. It is a block away from Case Western's Weatherhead School of Management, housed in an architectural wonder designed by Frank Gehry. Within walking distance are University Circle's Cleveland Museum of Art, Cleveland Natural History Museum, Museum of Contemporary Art, Cleveland Institute of Music, Cleveland Institute of Art, Cleveland Botanical Garden, and Severance Hall, home of the Cleveland Orchestra.

11401 Bellflower Rd.
216-791-7880
albatrosbrasserie.com

FIRE FOOD AND DRINK

Local market sources are just across Shaker Square

Douglas Katz, chef and owner of the fine-dining restaurant that everyone calls simply Fire, works the dining room like he likes it. Just as farmers teach him about food tastes, he says diners let him know what's working. The connection is gleeful, and he remembers patrons from previous visits. "Usually, you choose that table," says Katz, and the conversation buzzes from there.

Katz, who opened Fire in 2001 on Shaker Square and maintains a consistent high quality of cuisine and service, is a local leader in cooking with pasture-raised meats and sustainably raised fish. His motto, printed on the menu: "Simple food, sustainable practices, igniting the community."

Many a restaurant around the country talks of serving locally sourced products, but few of them are able to buy vegetables and fruit less than fifty yards away. Fire has a long list of food sources, but the closest is just outside the restaurant's front door at the Saturday morning North Union Farmers Market (see page 62). Just as the thriving market feeds meal makers in the neighborhood's apartments and nearby homes in Shaker Heights and Cleveland Heights, the kitchen at Fire gathers produce for use during the next week. How about syrup tapped from local maple trees?

"Seasonal ingredients taste so much better," says Katz, who has his own take on New American fare, designing menus of unexpected taste combinations in a variety of portion sizes. His creations (the menu changes a few times a season) might include chickpea fritters with cashew and mango chutney or crispy chicken liver with bacon among appetizers, and tandoor pork chop with spring pea succotash or whole rainbow trout with creamy leeks, crispy sunchokes, and caper-lemon relish, among entrées. A vegan entrée might be spring

Left: The patio at Fire on the sidewalk in Shaker Square.

Middle: Chef Douglas Katz in his open kitchen at Fire.

Right: The chef gets creative with spices and local products, such as this roasted tandoor chop with pork from Chardon, Ohio's New Creations Farm, sweet corn, and jalapeño spoonbread, local peach jam and sugar snap peas. (Photos courtesy of Fire Food and Drink)

pozole with smoky yellow pepper puree, hominy, sugar snap peas, rice, radish, peanuts, avocado, cactus salsa, cilantro, and tofu cotija.

The open kitchen is a focal point, visible from each table in the room of a 1929 building that faces a busy sidewalk and the trees of historic Shaker Square through big picture windows. The décor is natural colors and textures, fresh flowers, and lighting from an exposed ceiling. The patio on the front sidewalk is open in summer. Some inside tables are intimate for two, while other tables are closer together, which encourages small talk among diners. Every meal finishes with bite-sized complimentary chocolate chip cookies that come with the check.

The smallish bar is warm and friendly and serves from the regular menu. It's fun to come as a solo or couple and enjoy such dishes as a mushroom arugula salad with hazel nuts and Parmesan, a mushroom and Gruyère pizza with caramelized onions and herbs, and a side of spinach sautéed with shallots. The bar staff knows its wines, many available by the glass, and what will pair nicely with the food, which staff members have tasted. In 2012, Katz teamed with the Cleveland Museum of Art to oversee the Provenance restaurant at the museum.

13220 Shaker Square
216-921-3473
firefoodanddrink.com

61

NORTH UNION FARMERS MARKET

The city's top farmers market

Regular farmers markets dot the city, especially in summer, but the largest is in Shaker Square, where Cleveland meets Shaker Heights. The North Union Farmers Market is open on Saturday mornings, drawing a large, culturally diverse crowd. Farmers, food product creators, and artists sell goods from tents outdoors April to the week before Christmas and indoors in winter. The one big rule is that no dogs are allowed. While not required, most shoppers bring their own reusable bags.

You'll find some prepared foods and an occasional food truck, and there's a soapmaker and sometimes a guy who sharpens knives, but the real reason to come is fresh products, produce, fruit, and meats from Ohio farmers, including Amish families selling whatever is in season. You can also stock up on products from Ohio City Pasta, Cleveland Kraut, cheesemakers, and other local producers.

North Union was formed in 1995 by six area farmers, and all the growers who make appearances truck in their crops of corn, tomatoes, peaches, lettuce, apples, and more. Look for the gourmet

In late August, a season highlight is the market-sponsored Garlic Festival, a country fair complete with two days of cooking demos and garlic cookoffs (featuring local chefs), eating, beer drinking, live music, activities for children, and the crowning of a Miss Garlic (clevelandgarlicfestival.org). You'll know it's that time of year when a giant garlic "sculpture" goes up in Shaker Square. The idea of the festival, launched in 2008, was to help farmers get rid of their excess garlic crop.

Top left: Ohio City Pasta is among regular market purveyors, serving up fresh pasta in an impressive array of flavors.

Top right: Each Saturday morning, farmers such as Walnut Drive Gardens in Mogadore, Ohio, truck in whatever is fresh and in season.

Above left: Those with a sweet tooth, but little time to bake, will want to check out the prepared goods.

Above right: Organic Amish Country farms are among those represented at the weekly market.

mushroom grower if he's around! The square itself, which is actually shaped like a hexagon, is a historic landmark, with an RTA light rail train stop at the market (you cross tracks to get from one side of the market to the other).

Historic Shaker Square
216-751-7656
northunionfarmersmarket.org

EDWINS

Fancy French dining served by talented ex-cons

The birth and success of Edwins is a feel-good story. You enter this chic restaurant with a smile, aware of its unique approach to giving formerly incarcerated adults a foundation in the hospitality industry while providing a support network to help them successfully reenter the world outside and thrive. You leave the classy, white-tablecloth restaurant with another smile after a thoroughly satisfying meal with good music on the soundtrack—lots of Motown. Outdoor dining in summer spills out onto Shaker Square.

A French chef oversees the cuisine; ex-cons do the cooking and the serving, explaining the classic French menu, such as escargot, frog's legs with lots of garlic, duck confit, French cheese, and various wines that might accompany your choices. Meals tend to be a splurge.

Hospitality and culinary staff training comes from the Edwins Leadership & Restaurant Institute, which has grown from teaching in Ohio prisons in 2011 to opening the flagship restaurant in 2013. The Second Chance Life Skills Center, a 20,000-square-foot campus, opened nearby in 2016, offering students free housing, a library, and a workout facility with a basketball court. In December 2018, Edwins opened a butcher shop at 13024 Buckeye Road. The institute graduates more than a hundred students a year.

Brandon Edwin Chrostowski is the institute's founder and leader. He said the idea for Edwins was born from "a break" that he received early in life. For his efforts, Chrostowski was named a CNN Hero in 2017. He is a graduate of the Culinary Institute of America. He trained at some of the world's finer restaurants, became a certified sommelier, and was assistant general manager of L'Albatros in University Circle.

Edwins was showcased in 2018 in the Oscar-nominated documentary *Knife Skills*. Produced by three-time Oscar-nominated director and producer Thomas Lennon, the film focuses on reentry, second chances,

Top left: At Edwins you can create your own gourmet tasting plate, choosing from an impressive selection of artisan cheeses.

Top right: The kitchen line at Edwins.

Above left: Edwins' intimate dining room feels especially cozy in winter.

Above right: Brandon Edwin Chrostowski, founder and leader of the Edwins Leadership & Restaurant Institute. (Photos courtesy of Edwins)

and the power of food. To celebrate, the culinary team at Edwins prepared a dinner at the James Beard House in Manhattan to great applause and this report: "Cleveland's Edwins Restaurant draws diners for its lauded classic French fare, but the best things to come out of its kitchen may be the formerly incarcerated adults who receive hospitality and culinary training through the eatery's leadership institute."

The Edwins Institute's goal reaches beyond the kitchen and dining room to the community of Cleveland's vulnerable neighborhoods by providing its future leaders.

"In Cleveland, a sense of community is a priority," said Chrostowski, who once ran for mayor. "It's in our DNA. We know what we're fighting for. Volunteers don't just donate. They show up. We fight with time, talent, and treasures."

13101 Shaker Square
216-921-3333
edwinsrestaurant.org

BALATON RESTAURANT

Hungarian institution at Shaker Square

Just a peek inside Balaton and you can see that this restaurant fits its motto "Old World Hungarian Cuisine Since 1964." Two rooms with high ceilings and white walls look like a softly lighted, streetside eatery in Eastern Europe in 1964, with half-draped windows of Hungarian fabric, thin tablecloths, and a glass vase of simple flowers on each table.

Balaton's menu, perfect for a cold winter's day, is filled with a warm swath of selections of serious and delectable Hungarian food. Among the dinner specialties: bécsi szelet (breaded veal cutlet), cigánypecsenye (seasoned pork chops with garlic and paprika cream), and hortobágyi palacsinta (thin crepes of ground veal and mushrooms with paprikash gravy and sour cream). A group of two to four people at dinner might order fatányéros, which is a heavy wood platter of specialties.

The dinner menu is worth a study even after you have made a few choices to dine, as you might learn a Hungarian word or three. The lunch menu is simpler but no less filling: goulash, paprikash, stuffed cabbages, and Hungarian lecsó (thick vegetable stew). Portions are big. Half-portions are available on many entrées, all at moderate prices.

13133 Shaker Square
216-921-9691
balaton-restaurant.com

Top left: The dining room at Balaton looks out onto Shaker Square.

Top right: Antique dishes and furniture from Hungary greet diners at the entrance.

Bottom: Balaton is an intimate restaurant filled with reminders of the past. Not many restaurants today ask diners to sign a guest book.

Urban garden leads to a good story and a better martini

The late Margaret Mueller was seventy-nine when she bought a vacant side lot as part of a residential property sale in the city's Larchmere District. She wanted an urban vegetable garden—not so much the 1910 house—but the story goes that she bought them as a package and then turned the house and backyard patio into a family-run restaurant and neighborhood hangout. Mueller named the eatery Felice for two special women—her daughter, who owns clothing stores Plato's Closet and CLE Upscale Kids, and her granddaughter, who is a member of the U.S. Olympic rowing team.

The family says that Mueller's entrepreneurial spirit, love of a good story—and a better martini—shaped Felice, which has become a popular anchor among a string of restaurants that have renovated old homes and storefronts on Larchmere Avenue near Shaker Square. Felice began slowly as mostly an inside-the-house restaurant. It took off during a summer that the building's detached garage became a bar, and business moved outside. The martinis were popular. In winter, patrons gather inside the casual old Craftsman-style house, on the main floor with a fireplace, in the bar on the second floor, and in a lounge in the attic.

Felice's menu has a Mediterranean feel, with shared plates of fried calamari, sautéed brussels sprouts, chorizo and mushroom empanadas; small plates of mussels, grilled octopus, and grilled whole sardines; and large plates of zarzuela (chef's choice of fish), veggie kofta tacos, tofu with coconut rice, salmon with cauliflower puree, and pork poke bowl.

Grandmother's garden is expanding, providing veggies for the restaurant, say her grandson Jack Mueller and his husband, Paul Neundorfer, who now own Felice and have taken over its operation.

Top left: A Larchmere neighborhood house, built in 1910, is now a hot restaurant called Felice.

Top right: The perfect accompaniment to outdoor dining on a mild summer night is a pizza from the stone oven.

Above left: The warm-season bar fills an old detached garage.

Above right: A perpetual favorite at Felice is the crispy fried calamari.

They have added to the outdoor dining area, including a stone pizza oven. The menu, now with a Sunday brunch, has evolved, with new dairy-free, glutton-free, and vegan choices. Summer Thursdays bring live music to the patio.

The partners, who also own property in San Francisco, now spend much of their time in Cleveland, where Neundorfer is a cofounder of the Refugee Response, a nonprofit that "provides newcomers to the U.S. with education and employment training," he says. "We worked with local government agencies and the Refugee Response to design the Ohio City Farm, reported to be the largest contiguous urban farm in America." That farm, off West 25th Street in the Ohio City District, also provides vegetables for Felice.

12502 Larchmere Blvd.
216-791-0918
feliceurbancafe.com

BARROCO AREPA BAR

Recipes from a street cart in Colombia

Making real Colombian arepas is a three-day process that involves soaking, cooking, and grinding raw white hominy corn by hand. The resulting squares of dough (tortillas) are fried on a griddle, split open, and then stuffed with meat or vegetables. They are gluten free.

At the Barroco Arepa Bar on Larchmere Avenue near Shaker Square, diners have fifteen filling choices for this Colombian (and Venezuelan) street food as well as a wide variety of other Latin American dishes. Selections are served with a bunch of sauces in squeeze bottles, so you can tailor your flavors, whether you want a big dose of garlic, vegan pineapple salsa, or spicy peanut.

Barroco is a fun, lively, casual scene, with wooden tables and an eclectic décor, including whimsical artwork by the owner, Juan Vergara, and strings of colorful lights on the ceiling. Vergara's parents once owned a street cart in Colombia selling arepas, and Juan uses those recipes. After the family moved to the United States, Juan went to Cleveland State University, studying graphic design and marketing. He and his father, Carlos, launched the business.

All menu items at Barroco are made from scratch, including tasty stews and treats, such as fried pork rinds, sweet or savory plantains, and frijoles (kidney bean stew) with chorizo sausage made in-house. The arepas come with sides of French fries or yuca fries, tostones (fried plantains), black beans, red beans, plantains, or tortilla chips. Desserts include flan. The restaurant carries craft beers, some on tap, from local breweries and a house beer (passion fruit wheat, with the addition of fruit fermented in rum and triple sec). Mojitos, sangrias, margaritas, and piña coladas are on the drink menu, as are fresh-squeezed fruit juices without alcohol.

Top left: The back patio gets a crowd on warm summer nights.

Top right: Arepas are a popular menu option. Here, a grilled corn tortilla is topped with melted mozzarella, a charred beef patty, chimichurri and ranchero sauce.

Above left: Empanadas Colombianas are stuffed with braised beef and potatoes, served with ajisalsa.

Above right: The restaurant overlooks Larchmere, a neighborhood with a lively dining scene. (Photos courtesy of Barroco)

Brunches on weekends include eggs served with grilled arepas. Barroco also has a happy hour menu. In good weather, the art-filled outdoor patio, and—for people who like to watch passersby—a few tables on the street are open. Live music is scheduled for Monday and Friday nights, when diners are known to dance.

The Larchmere restaurant is a second location, following success in the West Side suburb of Lakewood, where Barroco began with twelve seats. The family opened a third Latin America eatery in Westlake.

12718 Larchmere Blvd.
216-938-9301
barrocoarepabar.com

Authentic Brazilian specialties in a renovated house

Four blocks of tree-lined Larchmere Boulevard, on Cleveland's East Side near Shaker Square, have become something of a foodie scene, home for a string of casual restaurants. Some are built into renovated Victorian houses, such as the one where Batuqui serves Brazilian specialties each evening for dinner.

Gustavo Nogueira and Carla Flood, both Brazilian, operate Batuqui as a comfortable, friendly gathering spot, like visiting someone's house for home-style Brazilian food cooked from recipes from both northern and southern Brazil. The restaurant opened in 2015.

In summer, the Larchmere street scene is thriving with outdoor tables on patios and porches. Batuqui fills front and back patios with twinkling lights and colorful umbrellas. When the weather gets colder, business shifts to a warm and welcoming interior.

The menu is authentic, homestyle cooking, with rich and flavorful dishes, such as a mixed grill of meats (including sausage) served with rice, farofa (a toasted cassava flour mixture), and tomato relish. Try feijoada, the Brazilian party stew of black beans and meats, including locally sourced bacon, ham, beef, smoked pork loin, smoked kielbasa, and linguiça, served with Brazilian rice, farofa, sautéed collard greens, and tomato. Xim xim, another stew, is shredded chicken, peanuts, and rice in coconut sauce. Batuqui's Bahia fish dish, mariscada, is based on a family recipe of Carla's and combines fish and shellfish cooked in a coconut milk sauce.

Most of the dishes are big flavored without being too spicy, but spice lovers may want to order the shrimp malagueta appetizer, which does pack some heat. Other appetizers include cod fish croquettes and stewed calamari. Also recommended: try the

Top left: Picanha Acebolada is tri-trip sirloin seasoned with sea salt, grilled and served with sautéed onions, rice and beans.

Top right: Seafood lovers will delight in Mariscada, a coconut milk-based seafood stew with calamari. mussels, shrimp, fish and crabmeat as well as sweet plantain.

Above left: Originating in Bahia, Brazil, Moqueca Baiana is a stew with a base of coconut milk, tomatoes and dende (palm) oil, and is served with rice. At Batuqui, it comes in shrimp, fish and vegetarian versions.

Above right: Churrasco de Picanha, a Brazilian steakhouse classic, satisfies carnivore cravings. (Photos courtesy of Batuqui)

Brazilian cheese bread, with its chewy, creamy qualities. Drinks include caipirnha, the Brazilian cocktail, which comes in traditional and strawberry varieties. You can order Brazilian soda and a plate of Brazilian tapas with your drink.

12706 Larchmere Blvd.
216-801-0227
batuquicleveland.com

BIG AL'S DINER

Classic for short-order breakfasts and lunches

Big Al is not that big nor is the restaurant, but the portions are. Waffles, for instance, cover the whole plate. Big Al's is a popular, inexpensive Larchmere neighborhood hangout for politicians and other folks hungry for breakfast from early morning to midafternoon. Cleveland's TV chef Michael Symon on Food Network's *The Best Thing I Ever Ate* says he judges a diner by its corned beef hash. For him, the best corned beef hash is at Big Al's. The hash is called "magic on a plate," with fresh green peppers, crispy corned beef, and a side of hand-cut hash browns.

Owners are medium-sized Al Windsor and his wife, Cheryl. "We serve food that is pesticide free," says Al. "We purchase our produce from the North Union Farmers Market at Shaker Square, and all of our ingredients are locally grown."

Neither the restaurant—checkerboard floor, red booths and stools, classic neon sign out front—nor the menu of comfort food is fancy, but the list of ways to have your eggs cooked is long and thorough. Specialties include eggs Benedict (with a vegetarian version); pancakes in a stack of one, two, or three (with a generous portion of whipped cream if you prefer); beef liver and onions, with or without house-made brown gravy; and corned beef sandwiches. Most dishes are less than ten dollars, and Big Al's is cash only. Breakfast is always available. At prime times, you may have to wait for a table but probably not too long.

12600 Larchmere Blvd.
216-791-8550
bigalscleveland.com

Big Al's is much warmer inside than it appears from the street. (Photo by Kristan Schiller)

LI WAH

Dim sum that wows

This three-hundred-seat restaurant opened in 1988, making it one of the earliest restaurants in the neighborhood known as AsiaTown. Founder Donna Hom wanted an authentic-style Chinese restaurant and a place that would bring the Chinese community together. "She wanted newcomers to have a place to go," says her son, Randy Ho, who now manages the operation along with other family members. Donna came to Ohio to marry Randy's father, who was from Youngstown. She opened Asia Plaza, the shopping mall where the restaurant is located. The family also has other restaurants outside the city.

Li Wah serves dim sum from 10:00 a.m. to 3:00 p.m. daily, but it is especially the place to be on weekends, when crowds come for an eye-popping array of small plates served from constantly arriving rolling carts and specialty items proffered from platters. You pay based on how many plates you devour—servers mark what you order on a tab at your table and then tally your total at the end of your meal. It's quick and high quality, and you can eat well for under twenty dollars per person.

The crowd is Chinese, pan-Asian, and everyone else who loves Chinese food, with big family groups not uncommon. There is a festive vibe, with diners sitting in black lacquer chairs at tables covered in white tablecloths. There's a regular menu, too, but why bother. Peruse

Asia Plaza is a multipurpose mall that is also home to Park To Shop, the city's best Asian market, with a particularly good fresh produce section and fish counter. Pick up giant bags of rice and stock up on such supplies as fish sauce and bamboo shoots. Within the mall are also shops selling porcelain bowls, Hello Kitty items, jewelry, and other Asian products, as well as a Chinese herbalist.

Left: The supermarket at Asia Plaza has an impressive array of produce, including Chinese eggplants.

Top middle: Wow your friends with roasted duck from the supermarket's meat department.

Bottom middle: The large dining room at Li Wah offers a dizzying array of dishes, staff arriving with carts and trays of dim sum and other favorites.

Right: Li Wah's steamed shrimp dumplings (front) are a fan favorite.

the carts and pick what looks good. You'll find the typical assortment of steamed buns, shrimp and pork shumai, steamed shrimp dumplings, sticky rice in lotus leaf, beef noodles, Chinese broccoli with oyster sauce, chicken feet with black bean sauce, and egg tarts. Li Wah makes ordering easy because your menu is your sheet, complete with photos.

The big surprise is what's on the trays. Randy, who grew up in Fairview Park, says they started with shrimp balls served fresh out of the fryer and got creative from there. You may be offered big glistening salt and pepper shrimp, chili crab, and even Peking duck. A chef visible near the entrance does the carving.

"The tray idea was my idea because of the fact you are able to offer something really different that no one else has or can even imagine doing," says Randy. Customers come from throughout the Cleveland area and from as far away as Pittsburgh, Cincinnati, and southern Indiana, Randy says. Yes, it's that good.

2999 Payne Ave.
216-696-6556
liwahrestaurant.com

LJ SHANGHAI

Shanghai-style soup dumplings in AsiaTown

Shanghainese soup dumplings are complicated to make and to eat. Edmond Tsui is a fan, and when he saw that Cleveland didn't have the dumplings, he decided to do something about that. Tsui, who had previously operated an Asian restaurant downtown, opened this casual dumpling shop in AsiaTown in 2018.

Soup dumplings are not an easy thing to pull off. The wrapper needs to be thick enough to hold the rich broth and filling but thin enough so you aren't getting a gob of dough. To get the soup and pork and chicken (or other) filling into the dumplings, you either freeze or gelatinize the flavorful broth and then carefully wrap. Tsui goes with the freezing method.

To show off the difficulty, Tsui has his kitchen visible behind glass. A video feed gives close-up views of the process. It's a similar setup to what you might find at a soup noodle shop in Shanghai or Singapore.

Cartoon illustrations show you how to eat the dumplings. You sip first and then eat the rest with house-made sweet vinegar. On the menu, too, are eggrolls, spicy Szechuan noodle soup, Shanghai-style noodles, and braised duck or pig ears for more adventurous diners.

3412 Superior Ave.
216-400-6936

Left: The bright and airy space is decorated with food posters.

Top right: Soup dumplings and Shanghai noodles are specialties of the house.

Above right: The dumpling shop opened in Asia Town in 2018. (Photos by Kristan Schiller)

NIGHTTOWN

Jazz, journalists, and lobster with Irish whiskey

Named after the Dublin red-light district in James Joyce's *Ulysses*, Nighttown is a retro white-tablecloth restaurant and lively tavern and one of the world's best-known jazz clubs. It is also home to the Press Club of Cleveland and the city's Journalism Hall of Fame, whose inducted members' plaques decorate some of the six rooms in the rambling restaurant.

Nighttown sits atop Cedar Hill within a five-minute drive of University Circle's museums, cultural and educational institutions, and the campuses of the city's two major learning and research hospitals. It is a favorite stop for commuters heading home to the Heights after work, couples enjoying a romantic evening, jazz lovers and musicians, and numerous travelers—from Wynton Marsalis to Stevie Wonder—who have dropped in for impromptu performances.

The 1920 building has long had at least a bit of a buzz. Once it was the Silhouette Lounge, run by mob-operated Cadillac Amusements until the feds shut it down. Nighttown arrived from the shadows in 1965 as a tavern, with an upright piano that occasionally drew a few local musicians. The restaurant was added in 1966, followed by two more bars and a year-round outdoor heated patio.

The mostly American menu, which is full, moderately priced, and available into the late night, seven nights a week, includes a classic favorite, the Dublin Lawyer, rich with lobster, whiskey, and cream, attractive for its reputation as suitable for the wealthy lawyers of Dublin and curious because the Irish were known as a people who seldom consumed seafood. The taste is similar to lobster Newburg, with plenty of butter and a good measure of Irish whiskey. Also popular are the classic trout amandine, the veal meatloaf, and the burger (made with Angus beef sirloin). The grilled halloumi (cheese) kabobs and whole steamed artichoke are among vegetarian options.

Left: The stage at Nighttown makes for intimate performances at one of the world's best known jazz clubs.

Middle: Walls at Nighttown are chocked full of posters, pictures, and the plaques of inductees to the Cleveland Journalism Hall of Fame.

Right: Entrance to Nighttown is off Cedar Avenue at the edge of Cleveland Heights, just up the hill from University Circle.

A key to planning dinner and which room to prefer when making a reservation is to check online or ask about the schedule for performances and their timing. For highly popular performers, tables may be packed tight in the main dining room, and as the show begins, folding chairs seem to appear in all available spaces. Other restaurant rooms are tucked away, the farthest being a large covered patio named Stephen's Green, after Dublin's best-known city park. The piano bar is open late on Friday and Saturday.

Owner since 2001 is Ireland-born Brendan Ring, who has expanded the restaurant and the stage area for musicians. Nighttown is on *DownBeat*'s list of the 100 Best Jazz Clubs in the World. A short list of performing alumni includes Count Basie, Freddy Cole, Jane Monheit, John Pizzarelli, Brian Auger, Ann Hampton Callaway, Tommy Tune, Ray Brown, Basia, Cyrille Aimee, Esperanza Spaulding, John Legend, Dick Cavett, and Dick Gregory.

12387 Cedar Rd.
216-795-0550
nighttowncleveland.com

INDIAN FLAME

Punjabi palate popular with the University Circle crowd

Don't be fooled by the colorless façade of this hole-in-the-wall Indian spot on Euclid Avenue near University Circle. The drab exterior belies what's inside: both a spicy feast for erudite taste buds and an unfailingly consistent Indian takeout frequented by nearby Case Western students and on-call doctors.

With seating for about thirty, Indian Flame has become a go-to for foodies seeking tasty, reasonably priced Indian fare since its opening in 2009 by Davinder and Baljinder Gill, both originally from Punjab in northwest India. Davinder, whose family had settled in Canada, moved to Cleveland in the mid-1990s to join Baljinder, whose family had settled in Cleveland. The couple live in Twinsburg with their two sons.

"We love it here," says Davinder. "We like the community, and we like the cold weather. Punjab is so hot! We're definitely staying."

Indian Flame's extensive menu includes vegetable samosas, butter chicken, and lamb vindaloo, as well as specialties such as goat curry (cooked in freshly ground spices, onion, and tomato gravy) and the Indian Flame mixed grill (chicken tikka, seekh kabob, and baby shrimp marinated in a tomato garlic sauce). The restaurant's garlic naan—a staple for Indian food lovers—is outstanding, sizzling, buttery, and loaded with fresh garlic.

A popular lunch buffet draws crowds daily so much so that the Gills are expanding in 2019 to a larger space nearby on Euclid Avenue next to the ice cream shop Piccadilly Artisan Creamery (piccadillycreamery.com). The space will seat fifty, says Gill, and has the added bonus of a bar, which is expected to appeal to the college kids.

Left: Co-owner Baljinder Gill may serve you the Mixed Grill, which arrives piping hot.

Right: The combo dish includes Chicken tikka, seekh kabob and baby shrimp marinated in tomato garlic sauce. (Photos by Kristan Schiller)

11623 Euclid Ave.
216-791-5555

HAPPY DOG (page 132)

BANTER (page 160)

WEST SIDE MARKET (page 146)

BARROCO AREPA BAR (page 70)

THE PLUM (page 186)

BREWNUTS (page 164)

GINKO (page 48)

NORTH UNION FARMERS MARKET (page 62)

THE FLYING FIG (page 128)

LARDER DELICATESSEN & BAKERY (page 140)

THE GREENHOUSE TAVERN (page 12)

FIRE FOOD AND DRINK (page 60)

CLEVELAND BAGEL COMPANY (page 126)

GITIZEN PIE (page 134)

SOHO CHICKEN + WHISKEY (page 192)

LI WAH (page 76)

MAMA SANTA'S

Sicilian-style Italian in Little Italy

Sometimes it's all about a great red sauce. So even though this restaurant in Little Italy may look like a dive out front, give it a chance. Inside there's a pervasive warmth that comes naturally to the waitstaff, many of whom are related. Mama Santa's has been doing its thing since 1961. Coming here for pizza or various forms of parmigiana is a classic Cleveland experience.

As you can quickly tell from the artwork on the walls, the family comes from Sicily. Guido Scaffidi served in the Italian Navy during World War II and was held prisoner by the Germans for three years before being rescued by the Americans. Shortly after the war, he and wife, Nancy, emigrated from Gioiosa Marea, Sicily, and settled in Akron before moving to Cleveland's Little Italy. He worked as an auto body repairman and she as a hairdresser. They brought the family recipes, including the outstanding sauce, so they opened their own ristorante.

Today, Case Western Reserve University students rub shoulders with multigenerational Italian families and everyone else seeking good, affordable Italian classics, including chicken cacciatore, homemade sausage, pastas, chicken or veal or eggplant parmigiana, and veal scaloppini. Pizzas are ordered as appetizers or as the whole meal—thin crust, saucy, cheesy, a little crunch where the crust is folded.

There's a short wine list, and if you have the right attitude, you'll be just as happy with the house white or red as anything else. No one is seeking quiet dining in two big rooms; children will feel comfortable here. Your waiter or waitress will put everyone at ease.

Part of the fun is that you can watch the pizza making going on out front, with windows from the street into the kitchen. The

Left: At Mama Santa's, you can watch the pizza makers toss the dough through a viewing window.

Right: The pizzas are popular as an appetizer or whole meal. You can build your own creation (from a list of toppings) or go with a specialty pie.

building itself is more than one hundred years old and earlier was a house, a bank, a clothing store, and a café.

Some may think Nancy is the mama, but the place was actually named in honor of her mother, Santa Ignazzito, who was born on All Saints Day November 1, 1908. She is the originator of the authentic recipes. Today, Guido and Nancy's sons, Anthony and Danny, are in charge. They've been working at the restaurant since they were teenagers and are assisted by Anthony's four children and various cousins. Anthony's wife, Pina, and her friend Angela, who is from Sicily, make all the homemade sauces, pastas, and dough.

12301 Mayfield Rd.
216-231-9567
mamasantas.com

CORBO'S BAKERY

A sweet taste of Italy, including cannolis

This family-owned bake shop in Little Italy (with other branches in and around the city) was opened in 1958 by Joseph and Antoinette Corbo. A third generation of family bakers continues the tradition, offering excellent versions of Italian sweets and some savory dishes too. A fourth generation also lends a hand. Load up on the best cannolis in town (plain or dipped in chocolate), choose from more than two dozen types of cookies and biscotti, or indulge in a pepperoni bread. You may also pick up prepared pizza dough and sauce.

Corbo's does wonderful, colorful birthday cakes that will wow children and adults. The bakery is known for its cassata cake—both the Cleveland version with layers of Italian sponge cake filled with custard, strawberries, and whipped cream, and the Sicilian version with rum-soaked cake and sweet ricotta filling. With donuts an in thing (see page 164), the family decided to bring back an old family recipe now for sale.

The Playhouse Square shop, opened in 2018, doubles as a café. Most of the baked goods are made in Little Italy and transported downtown, with donuts and bread made on-site.

The other popular bakery in Little Italy is Presti's Bakery (12101 Mayfield Rd.; 216-421-3060; prestisbakery.com), the place to stop if you're looking for a social café scene. Opened in 1902, the bakery has an array of baked goods, including breakfast pastries, breads and cookies (Italian and otherwise), cakes, pizza, and stromboli. They also offer sandwiches. Or just sit, chat, and people-watch over a coffee.

Left: Presti's Bakery is a Little Italy social scene for coffee and snacks (Photo by David G. Molyneaux)

Middle: Corbo's bakery creates extravagant cakes for weddings. (Photo courtesy of Corbo's Bakery)

Right: Corbo's glass cases are packed with more than two dozen varieties of cookies and biscotti. (Photo courtesy of Corbo's Bakery)

12210 Mayfield Rd. (Little Italy)
216-421-8181
corbosbakery.net

1603 Euclid Ave. (Playhouse Square)
216-400-7170

MIA BELLA RESTAURANT

Italian with a touch of Albania

A tad fancier than most other Little Italy eateries, Mia Bella has a welcoming and lively European bistro atmosphere, with exposed brick walls, white tablecloths and a big wooden bar. Some inside tables face big windows, so you can watch passersby on Little Italy's main street, Mayfield Road, where the restaurant has a few outdoor tables.

Chef Gerti Mehmeti was raised in Albania, and has helmed the kitchen at this family owned spot since it opened in 2010 when he was only 27. He already had experience in kitchens in Little Italy and elsewhere. His wife, Helga, does host duties.

While Italian dishes are featured on the menu, there's also a Mediterranean twist. Appetizers include shrimp *saganaki* and a chopped salad with feta and Kalamata olives. Mehmeti's veal braciola, a house specialty, is based on his own "secret ingredients."

Seafood comes in many preparations, including fresh oysters. Daily specials are based on what's in season, e.g., soft-shell crab on caviar pasta as a springtime treat. Rich lobster ravioli topped with white truffle oil is a popular choice. Spicy *frutti di mare piccanti* features shrimp, calamari and mussels. Mehmeti has also been known to whip up concoctions based on guest requests.

12200 Mayfield Rd.
216-795-2355
mblittleitaly.com

Top left: The restaurant occupies the first floor of a brick building in historic Little Italy. (Photo courtesy of Mia Bella)

Top right: Mia Bella is one of the neighborhood's more upscale restaurants. (Photo courtesy of Mia Bella)

Middle left: A specialty of the house is gnocchi alla Romana with tomatoes, Kalamata olives, onions, peppers, shallot and roasted garlic. (Photo courtesy of Mia Bella)

Above left: The atmosphere is lively bistro. The Mediterranean-focused menu includes some Albanian dishes. (Photo by David G. Molyneaux)

Right: Fresh oysters and a view of Mayfield Road, the main street in Little Italy. (Photo by David G. Molyneaux)

TOMMY'S RESTAURANT

Milkshakes in a hippy dippy community

Yes, it's a half mile outside the city into Cleveland Heights, but this hippie dippy throwback joint is a Cleveland institution. Generations have come to Tommy's in Coventry for thick milkshakes (including vegan versions) and casual eats. Started in 1972, Tommy's quickly gained attention when *Rolling Stone* magazine declared its ice cream creations Best Milkshake East of the Mississippi. The café moved to its current 125-seat location in 1993.

Many people order shakes, but the menu also cuts a wide swath in the casual food arena, whether you crave Middle Eastern food (hummus, spinach pie, falafel), a Seinfeldian "big salad," a great omelet, or a Reuben, made with either real corned beef or tempeh. They cater to all eating habits.

With free newspapers and flyers touting community events at the entrance and local artwork on the walls, Tommy's is a popular gathering spot for college students, families, and everyone else. Just put your name on the list at the counter and wait for a table.

1824 Coventry Rd.
216-321-7757
tommyscoventry.com

A cutout wall connects Tommy's to one of the best bookstores in town, Mac's Backs-Books on Coventry. The shop has three floors of new and used books to explore and hosts frequent author events.

Top left: Tommy's famous shakes to go come in regular and vegan versions.

Top right: The extensive menu includes Greek specialties such as falafel and deli sandwiches.

Above left: Owner and namesake Tom Fello, and some of his team.

Above right: Shakes are a source of pride at Tommy's. (Photos courtesy of Tommy's Restaurant)

HOT SAUCE LEGACY BBQ

Carrying on the famous BBQ tradition of Hot Sauce Williams

Once with five locations but now with two spinoffs on the East Side, Cleveland's iconic Hot Sauce Williams has been doing barbecue and Polish Boys since 1964. Lemaud Williams grew up in Tougaloo, Mississippi, and followed his four brothers to Cleveland, where they opened their first shop on Hough Avenue in 1964. "He had dyslexia and didn't figure he could make it in mainstream America. So, he decided to do his own thing," says his wife, Barbara, who runs the takeout only Superior Road shop, known as Hot Sauce Legacy BBQ (Lemaud died in 2013). The shop on Lee Road is run by another branch of the family.

The slow-cooked barbecue features a tangy, slightly spicy sauce and has won national awards. There's also fried chicken and shrimp on the menu as well as a popular Polish Boy. Here it's a baked, all-beef kielbasa topped with fries, coleslaw, and the BBQ sauce. If you want to get super sloppy, the Polish Girl adds an additional topping of pulled pork shoulder.

Over the years, boxing promoter Don King and Mike Tyson gave been among Hot Sauce Williams fans, and the enterprise was featured on both Anthony Bourdain's *No Reservations* and Travel Channel's *Man v. Food*.

Hot Sauce Legacy BBQ
12310 Superior Ave.
216-851-7788
facebook.com/Legacy-Barbecue-1491342391109274

Hot Sauce Williams
3770 Lee Rd.
216-921-4704

Top left: Hot Sauce Legacy BBQ serves recipes created by the Williams brothers, who opened their first barbecue joint in 1964.

Top right: Barbara Williams, wife of the late "Hot Sauce" Williams, operates Legacy with her son, Gregory.

Middle left: The Polish Boy is messy and delicious.

Above left: Slow-cooked barbecue, fried chicken and shrimp, and Polish Boys are on the menu at the takeout only Superior Road location.

Above right: Hot Sauce Williams gained fans locally and nationally, including winning barbeque competitions. (Photo courtesy of Barbara Williams)

GALLUCCI'S ITALIAN FOODS

Where Clevelanders stock up on authentic Italian goods

In Cleveland's Midtown Corridor between downtown and University is this oasis for all things Italian. The legacy of the shop dates back to the early 1900s when Gust Gallucci, an immigrant from Faeto, Italy, started selling goods from a wooden cart and later opened a neighborhood grocery store on the West Side. Gust's sons, Frank and Ray, joined the business, and while the location changed a few times, Gallucci's is still going strong as a family-owned enterprise. The supermarket-sized retail shop is open to the public, while the massive wholesale warehouse out back supplies local restaurants.

Gust's concept was both good food and a gathering place for the local Italian community, says his grandson, Ray Jr., who runs the operation today (a fourth generation of the family is involved too). The store hosts such events as the annual (in November) Cutting of the Crucolo cheese, signaling the start of the holiday season.

Gallucci's is the place to go for a big choice of prosciuttos and other Italian cold cuts, including direct-from-Italy items, such as salami and capicola that you can't find elsewhere in the city. At the deli counter, a big choice of domestic and imported cheeses

Gust Galluci's legacy includes recognition for the business from the City of Cleveland in 2012, with Mayor Frank Jackson honoring the one-hundredth anniversary with a proclamation. A centenary plaque was also dedicated. The Italian government recognized Ray Jr. with a Distinguished Service Award from the Italian Trade Commission in 2010.

Left: In addition to foodstuffs, Gallucci's has impressive wine selections.

Right: The deli counter has an eye-popping array of direct-from-Italy cold cuts and domestic and imported cheeses.

is available, including Parmigiano Reggiano and balls of fresh mozzarella.

Head to the back of the store and your stomach will no doubt start rumbling with the smell of onions and peppers on the grill. Don't bother trying to resist an eggplant parm, Italian sausage, or meatball sandwich. They are delicious. In decent weather, you can eat your lunch outdoors on the picnic benches.

Just don't get so caught up in your meal that you forget to peruse the shelves, refrigerator, and frozen food cases. You can bring home a frozen lasagna or pasta made in-house or all the ingredients you need to make pizza (including Mama Gallucci's sauce); stock up on olive oil, the selection including Gallucci's own EVOO label; buy cans of imported Italian canned tomatoes; and choose from the impressive array of balsamic vinegars. If you're not watching calories, stop by the bakery counter for a cannoli, and pick up fresh baked bread while you're there.

In a nod to the local Hungarian community, Gallucci's also stocks items imported from Hungary, including paprika and Hungarian-style salami. The store also has an extensive wine selection, including many Italian labels.

6610 Euclid Ave.
216-881-0045
tasteitaly.com

SIAM CAFE

Family-run business with a menu of one hundred items

Sometimes a favorite eatery slips your mind for a while. Then you'll be talking with friends about where to go for dinner. You mention some choices without agreement until someone says "Siam Cafe," and everyone nods yes. Since 1994, the pan-Asian Siam Cafe has been a go-to restaurant for foodies, chefs on their day off, pre-theater and after-theater meals, and diners who love the impressive array of Thai, Chinese, and Vietnamese specialties from a menu that numbers about a hundred items.

Siam Cafe sits unobtrusively at East 40th and St. Clair at the eastern edge of the growing Asian community's food stores and eateries. Free parking is plentiful around an ordinary-looking building with a large, simple dining room (if you think it looks a bit like an old Denny's, it was). Don't let any of this fool you into passing by. The restaurant is white tablecloth and full service, staffed with experienced cooks and waiters—owner Michael Hong employs a host of family members from several generations—open daily until midnight. The family will make you feel welcome, and while there often seems to be a big crowd in this bustling restaurant, a free table is available somewhere.

Live lobsters move in the tank in the back of the room, which is reason enough to order lobster with ginger and green onion or lobster with garlic sauce. You may order Peking duck by calling in advance or take your chances that duck buns are available, off the menu. The braised pork leg (ham hock) feeds at least several people. Other favorites include Singapore-style stir-fried vermicelli with shrimp and chicken, whole black bass, shrimp wonton soup, and

Top left: Dishes appeal to a variety of tastes. The Fish Fillet in Szechuan Hot Oil Broth packs some heat. (Photo courtesy of Siam Café)

Top right: The restaurant occupies a building that was originally a Denny's.

Above left: The uniformed waitstaff helps diners choose selections from a huge pan-Asian menu.

Above right: The stuffed chicken wings are a favorite of foodie patrons, including Cleveland Chef Zack Bruell.

Siam wings (three big chicken drumettes per serving, stuffed). Many dishes are served on sizzling pans.

Best to gather a group of four or more so that everyone gets numerous tastes. It doesn't matter how many items you order because waiters are gracious about packaging up leftovers to take home. Make certain to add an order of snow pea shoots (or other green vegetables) with garlic, which may turn out to be your favorite dish on the menu, but don't ask for fortune cookies or the waiter will remind you that the Siam Cafe is not a Chinese restaurant.

3951 St. Clair Ave.
216-361-2323
facebook.com/SiamCafe

SUPERIOR PHO

Casual spot serves the best pho in town

Clevelanders have been warming up over steaming bowls of pho (pronounced "fuh"), the Vietnamese noodle soup, since this bustling family-run restaurant opened in 2002. It's located in a nondescript shopping mall in AsiaTown, but no one cares. The fragrant, award-winning pho here is based on old family recipes from Vietnam, and it's delicious.

Owner Manh Nguyen left Saigon for Cleveland in 1975, sponsored by a local church. He worked in a steel mill, married, and eventually earned a degree and moved up to metallurgist. A passionate food lover, it bothered him there was no good Vietnamese food in town.

"We used to get in the car and drive six hours to Chicago for pho and then drive six hours home," says son, Chris Nguyen, who was raised in the Old Brooklyn neighborhood. Manh decided to mortgage his home and open his own restaurant, with recipes from his grandmother for inspiration. It was a bold move, since Clevelanders at the time weren't known for their willingness to try new things.

At Superior Pho, meats and spices, including ginger and cinnamon, simmer for some twenty-four hours to create the broth, the most important ingredient in pho. The broth is carefully ladled into bowls with rice noodles and topped with tender slices of eye-round steak or beef brisket or both. For those who don't eat red meat, chicken, vegetarian, and other varieties are available too.

A wine aficionado, Manh likes to compare his broth to wine—the nose, the body, the finish.

Left: The décor is simple, the flavorful pho broth anything but.

Right: The easiest entrance to Superior Pho is from a parking lot behind the Superior Avenue restaurant.

All are served with the traditional accompaniments of fresh bean sprouts, basil, lime wedges, and slices of jalapeño peppers, as well as hoisin and hot sauces you can add to taste. The restaurant also serves a wonderful banh mi sandwich, with the roast pork, pâté, and mayonnaise all made in house.

The décor is simple, but you may not notice. The steaming bowl in front of you will grab your attention. Both Manh and Chris do the cooking. Chris, who graduated from Bowling Green University in 2010, came up with the idea to start selling Superior Pho T-shirts—created by Cleveland artist/designer Glen Infante—and they've become a popular item. Finding Superior Pho can be a challenge—the best entrance is from the parking lot—but the "secret" status adds to the allure. Don't be put off if you see long lines into the hallways of the mall; they move fast.

3030 Superior Ave. E
216-781-7462
superiorpho.com

SZECHUAN GOURMET

Hidden gem for spice lovers

For those who like things hot, or at least full of flavor, this hidden, no-frills gem serves up a huge menu that is heavy on Szechuan peppercorns and dried chilies but also includes plenty of non-spicy dishes for your friends who prefer milder dining.

Ignore the unattractive entrance off a parking lot next to the Tink Holl Asian market (which is also worth a look). Come ready to explore. The menu, in both English and Chinese, has more than three hundred authentic dishes, some with ingredients you've probably never heard of. Be aware that the star rating system for spicy is pretty accurate—level three is hot!

Chinese food fans with an adventuresome spirit will be delighted to find such dishes as chilled beef tendon in chili sauce and salt and pepper frog. Try various delicious hotpots with simmering broth and dry pots without the broth, and such favorites as pan-fried pork dumplings, scallion pancakes, roast duck, and kung pao chicken as well as two dozen noodle dishes. Portions are huge; you'll likely take some home.

1735 E. 36th St.
216-881-9688
facebook.com/pages/category/Szechuan-Sichuan-Restaurant/
Szechuan-Gourmet-258602604242428/

川味軒
Szechuan Gourmet

Seafood
Hot Pot
KTV

Top: The menu at Szechuan Gourmet features more than 300 authentic dishes.

Above: The peppers on the restaurant sign assure spice-lovers they will find their cravings satisfied, with milder dishes also available. (Photos by Kristian Schiller)

BRATENAHL KITCHEN

Big portions of Jamaican comfort food

Lovers of jerk chicken and other authentic Jamaican food drive to North Collinwood, just off Interstate 90, to pick up their take-out dinner. The face of this kitchen is a hole in a wall covered by a bulletproof window, though there is a table inside as well as a few tables on the covered patio outside.

It's a modest spot. Look for a little yellow-and-green shack. Pick from a hand-lettered chalkboard. The chef takes and cooks your order and provides big portions of Jamaican comfort food with pimento-based seasoning, mostly garlic, onions, and peppers. Try the braised oxtail, hearty stews of chicken or goat curry, Jamaican beef pies (called patties), spicy jerk chicken, and island-style catfish. Sides include rice and beans, steamed cabbage, mac & cheese, and fried plantains. Try a Ting (Jamaican grapefruit soda).

In a small storefront nearby, Ocho Rios True Island Cuisine offers a similar menu.

Bratenahl Kitchen
14002 Lakeshore Blvd.
216-383-1874
facebook.com/pages/Bratenahl-Kitchen/191259094369714

Ocho Rios True Island Cuisine
1007 Ivanhoe Rd.
216-249-6246
ochoriostrueislandcuisine.com

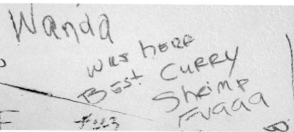

Top left: A simple front door off Lakeshore Boulevard leads to the order room, where patrons waiting for their food have filled the white walls and ceiling with their names and thoughts of the moment. Customers are not welcome inside the locked door to the kitchen.

Top right: The modest Bratanahl Kitchen has a few outdoor tables for waiting in warm weather.

Middle right: A citizen review from a customer named Wanda, who likes the curry shrimp. "Best evaaa," she wrote.

Above left: The cook, Rich Richards, in his kittchen.

Above right: The menu: chicken, fish, specialties, wings, sides, Jamaican pop, desserts.

LE PETIT TRIANGLE CAFE

Leave pretenses at the front door at this casual French café

Owners of this warm, intimate French café in the Ohio City neighborhood see their success as community driven. They provide a homey sort of place where folks might walk a few blocks for a bowl of French onion soup and a glass of wine or perhaps expand the evening into a dinner of several courses.

Conversations overheard around the six-table patio out front indicate that diners also come from neighborhoods much farther away because, they said, even a big American city has few authentic French cafés. One man said he drove across town specifically for the escargot, which was served with garlic parsley butter and enough crusty French bread to sop up the butter that remained in the serving dish after the six snails had been consumed.

Le Petit Triangle was patterned after a café in Paris. The décor says French in a comfortable, casual way, and the place looks like one you might find in France. It is a fine stop for a fresh croissant and espresso in the morning, a crepe over a meeting at lunch, or an evening hangout with friends and family, enjoying food and beverages indigenous to the French-European culture.

"People come in and out for as little as forty minutes or stay as long as three hours," says Tom Harlor, who, with his wife, Joy, have owned the restaurant since 2006. "We have expanded the menu," says Tom. "We began as a creperie in one room. We didn't have squat. Now we have squat."

Savory crepes remain on the menu, with white or buckwheat flour. Recently, they included chicken cheddar and chutney; smoked salmon with spinach, red onion, and capers; and two vegetarian choices, one with spinach tomato, chevre, and olive tapenade and the

Left: The intimate dining room at Le Petit Triangle Cafe in Ohio City is a reminder of eating in France.

Right: French three onion soup with gruyere croute, vegetarian based.

other of mushrooms, bleu d'Auvergne cheese, caramelized onions, and scrambled eggs. You can enjoy yummy dessert crepes too.

For a small restaurant, the menu choices are many. You'll find standards, such as boeuf bourguignon, cassoulet, chicken with ratatouille, and bouillabaisse. Stock is made from scratch. The French wine list is extensive, with about twenty by the glass, and a nice selection of cheeses is also available.

"We have a theme," says Joy Harlor. "Stay with what you are. We hold the line on prices and leave pretenses at the door. This is about longevity. Our first two servers still work here. We make eye contact with diners." The Harlors live four blocks from the restaurant in their home of twenty years. They are lifelong Northern Ohioans.

1881 Fulton Rd.
216-281-1881
lepetittriangle.com

ASTORIA CAFE & MARKET

Mix and mingle with gourmets and gourmands at this lively café

A well-established wholesale company, Agora Foods International decided to branch out into retail in late 2016. Owners opened this bright café and shop directly in front of their twenty-thousand-square-foot warehouse near Gordon Square. The result is a trendy gourmet wonderland. Astoria was quickly embraced as an oasis where Cleveland foodies can be part of a lively and creative dining scene, meet and mingle, drink good wine (including French and Italian selections) and beer or craft cocktails, and bring home high-quality products to wow their own dinner guests. The café side focuses on shareable plates, charcuterie boards, and pizza, using Mediterranean and local ingredients.

The chef de cuisine is Cory Kobrinski, who learned the craft working at other Ohio restaurants and also happens to be an award-winning saxophonist. He has what some of his peers may envy—a whole warehouse of ingredients to play with. Agora also supplies other restaurants in town, but he can just walk out back and pick what he needs.

Kobrinksi gives a big nod to the health-focused Mediterranean diet, though he also ventures into richer territory in some of his well-imagined concoctions. You'll need to decide whether you are in the mood for dolmades (stuffed grape leaves) or French-baked brie en croute, whether you feel like a board with Serrano ham or prosciutto

Astoria Cafe is named for a neighborhood in Queens, New York, that has a large Greek population. Astoria, Queens, got its name from millionaire John Jacob Astor as part of a business deal.

124

Left: Top-quality take home goods line the shelves at Astoria Café & Market.

Right: The lively café is popular with the foodie crowd, who come to sample a wide range of Mediterranean favorites.

di Parma. Pizza toppings might include wild mushrooms or veal and lamb meatballs.

Guests sit at high tops or low tables, with views of Detroit Avenue, or at the marble bar, with views of the open kitchen. Coming with a crowd so that you can share more dishes is recommended. The staff is good at making suggestions, including how many dishes to order.

Local ingredients make appearances, such as Ohio City Pasta and local Ohio corn on the cob. Weekend brunches are particularly popular: you can splurge on such choices as breakfast pizza, sea scallop and crab eggs Benedict, or duck confit and hash.

Wander over to the market to choose take-home cheeses from France, Italy, and all over Europe and a selection of cured meats and pâtés from top purveyors, such as Schaller & Weber and Leoncini. Private label Mediterranean Artisan brand products include capers, roasted red peppers, tahini, pepperoncini, dolmades, and Greek olives. On metal shelves, you'll find displays of EVOO from several countries, including Mediterranean Artisan-label from Crete, as well as such delightful surprises as Austrian pumpkin seed oil. There's also a wide selection of olives, grains, rice, beans, and pasta.

5417 Detroit Ave.
216-266-0834
astoriacafemarket.com

CLEVELAND BAGEL COMPANY

City gets a bagel thanks to "Cleveland Hustles"

This bagel maker set out in 2016 to create a distinctive Cleveland gourmet bagel much like New York and Montreal have their own versions. Partners Dan Herbst and Geoff Hardman got a substantial boost from LeBron James and his CNBC show *Cleveland Hustles*, which focused on business ideas for the Gordon Square-Detroit Shoreway neighborhood, walking away from the show with a check for $100,000.

The bagels are small with a small hole and take twenty-four hours to make. They are hand-rolled, slowly fermented, boiled in water, and baked. The result is a crisp exterior plus a good chewy interior. Flavors go traditional and not, for example, rosemary sea salt, and are paired with such inventive spreads as thyme black pepper horseradish and brie honey walnut. Bagel sandwiches are available, too, including with house-made lox.

You'll wait in a line with dozens or even hundreds of other fans to get a taste. Plans are in the works to open a second location and production facility on the East Side. The bagels are featured at local coffee houses and restaurants Nighttown and the Flying Fig.

4201 Detroit Ave.
216-600-5652
clebagelco.com

Top left: The gourmet Cleveland bagels are small, with a small hole in the center.

Top right: Bagel sandwiches are on the menu, including egg and cheese, hummus and avocado and classic lox, with house-made lox. (Photo courtesy of Cleveland Bagel Company)

Above: Cleveland Bagel Company was opened with the help of LeBron James and his CNBC show *Cleveland Hustles*.

THE FLYING FIG

James Beard-nominated farm-to-table cuisine

In 2018, two women chefs made Cleveland proud as semifinalists for the James Beard Award for Best Chef: Great Lakes. Chef Karen Small, a longtime local favorite, was one of them (see also Chef Jill Vedaa on page 144).

Working from a friendly little Ohio City restaurant, Small embraces the fresh, locavore spirit with big flavors on creative plates where ingredients shine. Some dishes might display an Italian or Asian influence; nothing is too pretentious. The idea is cuisine that is approachable for both those seeking new flavors and those less adventurous about their food choices. A popular dish, for instance, is the chicken schnitzel sandwich with rosemary fries and house ketchup. Small also does a great burger, using grass-fed Miller Livestock beef.

The menu changes seasonally, and you might in summer find a special of a summer green salad with local honey in the dressing or ribs made with rhubarb BBQ sauce. Her Taleggio polenta might be topped with locally grown mushrooms and fresh vegetables, or she may go in a completely different direction.

Small opened her restaurant in 1999 after working at other local eateries. Sustainable agriculture has always been a focus, as has giving back, including teaching cooking classes to encourage healthy eating to children and the financially challenged. Local providers are listed on the Flying Fig website, including Mackenzie Creamery, Killbuck Family Mushrooms, North Union Farmers Market, and Mitchell's Ice Cream.

The décor is as approachable as the food, lanterns topping the L-shaped bar, modern art together with farm artifacts displayed on the walls, and a little patio out front, which happens to be right across the street from the Great Lakes Brewing Company. The wine list is small but diverse, including half bottles for under twenty dollars.

Top left: At The Flying Fig, you'll experience big flavors in dishes such as trout curry.

Top right: The restaurant has been a fixture in Ohio City since 1999, long before the neighborhood was deemed trendy.

Above left: James Beard-nominated Chef Karen Small believes in sustainable agriculture and giving back to the community. (Photos by Karin McKenna, courtesy of Flying Fig)

Small does a popular brunch on Saturdays and Sundays, with such options as huevos rancheros with confit chicken, lemon and blueberry pancakes, and an Ohio brunch burger topped with a fried egg. Bread gets a prominent place on the menu, and you can buy take-home loaves along with Flying Figs's homemade pickles, jams, pastries, carry-out food options, and more at the store next to the restaurant, Market at the Fig, which also stocks craft beers, wine, charcuterie, and artisanal cheeses. The Flying Fig regularly hosts wine dinners and also does a Farmers Market Seasonal Supper Series.

2523 Market Ave.
216-241-4243
theflyingfig.com

GREAT LAKES BREWING COMPANY

Craft breweries pair suds with good grub

Breweries' bread and butter is what's poured into your glass. Some brewers also provide menus to keep their customers quaffing on the premises. In 1988, Pat and Dan Conway opened Great Lakes Brewing Company, Ohio's first craft brewery. It has evolved to be the thriving anchor in the Ohio City District west of downtown just across the Cuyahoga River.

Great Lakes, which is Ohio's largest craft brewery, is both a tourist destination and a place of pilgrimage for craft beeries—the beer version of foodies. A one-hour tour, conducted beer in hand (bring your ID), includes the tiger mahogany bar where Eliot Ness, leader of "The Untouchables" in Chicago and later Cleveland Safety Director, once sat. The Great Lakes food menu features brewer's barley pretzels, made from spent grain, and burgers from spent-grain fed cows. Greens are grown at a nearby farm. Short ribs are braised with Edmund Fitzgerald Porter.

At Noble Beast Brewing Co. just east of downtown, brewer Shaun Yasaki and chef James Redford pair their talents in a lively taproom shared with impressive brewhouse equipment in a brick warehouse. The food is as thoughtful as the classic beers, including seasoned popcorn and burgers with a meat-emulation patty. Redford says, "I wanted to put the whole beer thing into the food." Spent grain is in the bread. The veggie sandwich is an amalgamation of cucumbers, radishes, pickled beets, arugula, white cheddar, almond butter, and garlic aioli.

Ohio City's Hansa Brewery makes a variety of beers, and many, such as Kölsch, Oktoberfest, and Schwarzbier, are light enough

Left: The basement bar has that old cellar hideaway feel.

Middle: Lunch at Great Lakes beside working brewery equipment.

Right: One of Great Lakes' most popular craft beers is named for former Clevelander Eliot Ness, once safety director and local candidate for mayor who gained fame in Chicago in *The Untouchables*

to pair with heavier dishes on the menu, such as a sausage platter, schnitzel, and a mixed grill of čevapi and ražniči. The Hansa Import Haus is next door.

The cavernous Masthead Brewing Co., housed in a former car dealership on Superior Avenue, has a menu of more than twenty pizzas, ranging from vegan to Spanish chorizo, from a Neapolitan wood-fired oven. Each of these tasty bites is paired with a beer from a rotating list. The brewery won a Great American Beer Festival medal.

Great Lakes Brewing Company
2516 Market Ave.
216-771-4404
greatlakesbrewing.com

Masthead Brewing Co.
1261 Superior Ave.
216-206-6176
mastheadbrewingco.com

Hansa Brewery
2717 Lorain Ave.
216-631-6585
hansabrewery.com

Noble Beast Brewing Co.
1470 Lakeside Ave.
216-417-8588
noblebeastbeer.com

HAPPY DOG

Hot dogs, cocktails, live music, and community

Happy Dog isn't just a dining spot. It's a Cleveland institution. Hot dogs with wild toppings are on the menu, along with tater tots and fries with more toppings and beer. But this is a place where you can hear a noted professor lecture on physics, dance the polka, participate in a poetry reading, or compete in a pinball tournament. Come for lunch or dinner or late at night. It's open into the wee hours. The ambience is classic neighborhood bar—only on steroids.

The décor might make you feel like you're back in the 1940s celebrating the end of the big war. You can sit at the chrome barstools and belly up to a wooden bar.

The live music that happens here is across the board, with rock, country, punk, soul, and karaoke. Members of the Cleveland Orchestra perform once a month; in fact, there's a double vinyl recording called *Ensemble HD Live at the Happy Dog* that combines some of those performances.

Chef Eric Williams of Momocho (see page 142) helped come up with the menu. The all-beef hot dogs are made locally by Blue Ribbon Meats from a Happy Dog recipe. The Artisan Vegan Sausage is produced by Field Roast and imported from Seattle. They are served in buns made by Cleveland's Orlando Baking Company. Choose from some fifty toppings for the dogs/vegan sausages (and Thursday burgers too), whether you're in the mood for bourbon pork-n-beans, SpaghettiOs, Froot Loops, or marinated cremini mushrooms. The tater tots and fries come with a choice of forty toppings.

While you're munching, you may hear a talk by folks from Case Western Reserve University or other area institutions—scientists, writers, and experts on various subjects. The place is like the neighborhood bar on *Cheers* with the added bonus of intellectual

Left: The menu takes creativity with junk food to new realms. Patrons can choose from a wide array of hot dog toppings. including a particular multi-colored, sugary breakfast cereal.

Top right: The dose of culture includes various genres of music.

Above right: A Cleveland institution, Happy Dog is as much a hangout spot as a place to eat. (Photos courtesy of Happy Dog)

conversation. Physics and science are popular themes for lectures. You might find Glenn Starkman, Distinguished Professor at Case Western Reserve, talking about the state of the universe. There are also events sponsored by the Cleveland Council on World Affairs. Storytelling shows and trivia nights are part of the scene too.

The menu of seventy-five beers includes craft beers and imported selections from Slovenia, Poland, the Czech Republic, and elsewhere in Eastern Europe. At any given time, more than twenty beers are available on tap.

5801 Detroit Ave.
216-651-9474
happydog.com

CITIZEN PIE

Going for the perfect Naples-style pizza

"Pizza for the people"—the words displayed with a raised fist—is the logo for this pizza shop. It's your first hint that something unusual might be taking place. The shop is the brainchild of Vytauras Sasnauskas, who moved to Cleveland from Lithuania and has an acknowledged obsession with pizza. Growing up in the Soviet Union, he didn't eat pizza until he was twelve, and the Lithuanian version he experienced was topped with a hard-boiled egg and olives. But he got hooked.

After attending culinary school in Lithuania, he moved to Cleveland in 1996. He says he learned English by reading cooking books. With a dream of making pizzas, he traveled to Naples to learn more about dough and ovens and such. Lucky for him, his mentor was Franco Pepe, one of Italy's top pizza pros.

Back in Cleveland, Sasnauskas put together a wood-fired oven lined with volcanic stone "from the foothills of Mount Vesuvius." His dough is fresh daily, made with Italian milled flour, salt from Italy, and Cleveland water (he carefully guards what he uses as a starter). The oven is fired with apple, oak, and cherry wood. His optimum temperature for cooking is 900°F, which allows the exceptionally thin crust to cook in about ninety seconds.

The Collinwood location is a hole-in-the-wall joint with limited seating—the best spot being the stools that overlook the street—one

Sasnauskas can wax poetic about pizza making. "It's a very, very, very difficult form of cooking because it is less ingredients. Like wine. What is wine? Grape juice. So how do you make great wine. It's the same with pizza. You can be the best chef in the world and still not make good pizza."

Left: Naples-style pizza is cooked at 900°F to create a tasty, slightly crusty crust.

Middle: Specialty pies include Cacio de Pepe, with mozzarella, stracciatella and Percorino cheese, garlic, black pepper and basil.

Right: The Ohio City location is larger than the original hole-in-the-wall spot in Collinwood.

wall covered with icons, including Karl Marx and Jimi Hendrix. Most people do takeout. The Ohio City location is newer, bigger, and trendier. Online, a meter shows how much pizza dough is left. It's worth checking before you leave home, as sometimes he does run out of dough.

Toppings help boost the pizza into the stratosphere. A favorite is the cacio e pepe with mozzarella, straciatella, garlic, black pepper, and pecorino. Even a simple marinara, without mozzarella but with oregano, garlic, basil, and pecorino, is impressive. The house Citizen Pie combines ricotta, mozzarella, salami, and basil, or order from the selection of other red and white pizzas and calzones. In Ohio City, you can also order pies topped with salad and house-made, soft-serve ice cream for dessert.

15710 Waterloo Rd.
(across the street from the Beachland Ballroom music venue)
216-417-2742

2144 W. 25th St.
216-860-1388
citizenpie.com

BAR CENTO

Open late among the pack of thriving Ohio City pubs

It's midnight, and you are hungry. Cleveland is an early-rising city (the freeways are packed at 6:30 a.m.) but until the past decade or so not so much a late-eating place. The addition of new downtown residents, including thousands of young people, has changed the late-night eating scene, with at least a dozen choices within easy access from downtown. Bar Cento, in the Ohio City District, is a popular, casual gastropub, especially lively from happy hour to 2:30 a.m. daily, serving food until 2:00 a.m.

Co-owner Sam McNulty, Bar Cento's founder, grew up in Cleveland Heights and opened his first restaurant while a junior at Cleveland State University. He describes the menu as elevated bar food, with a focus on modern Italian. The twice-fried pommes frites are a favorite, with garlic and rosemary, served with dollops of curry, garlic, and red pepper aioli—ketchup on the side. Try the Belgian beer-steamed mussels; a big board loaded with house-cured meats, cheeses, and pickles to share with friends; and a pizza with three sunnyside-up Blue Loon Farm eggs, provolone, and house-made pancetta. The Sunday brunch includes a house-made sausage sandwich, tiramisu French toast, and creamy polenta topped with an egg.

The sixteen-seat bar was built with reclaimed wood from an Amish barn. The wine list is extensive and so is the collection of Scotch. Bar Cento plans frequent Scotch, wine, and beer tastings. On tap are local craft beers. Next door is the sister Bier Markt, serving more than a hundred Belgian and American craft beers. McNulty also owns the nearby Market Garden Brewery. When the weather is good, plan to sit at sidewalk tables or on the patio.

Left: Bar food ranges from pizza to tiramisu French toast of challah, espresso, mascarpone whipped cream.

Right: Check the board on W. 25th Street and the website for events, including beer specials, wine and scotch tastings.

There's always something to ward off those late-night hunger pangs in the Ohio City neighborhood, which is just across the Cuyahoga River from downtown, a five-minute Uber drive from Public Square, a thirty-minute walk in good weather, and a five-minute stroll from the West 25th Street light rail station.

1948 West 25th St.
216-274-1010
barcento.com

THE BLACK PIG

Gastropub where pigging out takes on new meaning

As you might expect in a restaurant called The Black Pig, Ohio pork owns a major portion of the dinner menu as well as the popular weekend brunch. Chef Michael Nowak is an expert on braising, which shows throughout his European-inspired, New American cuisine that is seasonal and locally sourced. He uses the whole pig, even the collar, and there are non-pig choices too.

Black Pig is a cozy place, with a small but lively bar, brick walls, tile floors, and a dark elegance in an Ohio City neighborhood building that once held a restaurant called Parker's, by pioneering chef Parker Bosley. Diners eat in the dining room, two private rooms upstairs, and on the patio in good weather.

At brunches, sweet, thick bacon gets showcase treatment, topped with sugar and bruléed with a blowtorch. The brunch menu also includes corned chicken livers and a "Free Range Toad in a Hole" (egg, toast with brie cheese and black truffle).

At dinner, the menu changes nightly—and sometimes more often—if something special becomes available from a nearby market. Among the pork possibilities, you might find chili cheese pork rinds with Fresno chili hot sauce and Parmesan; pork belly with spelt dumplings, grain mustard cream and beet glaze; spiced pork meatballs with freekah and chickpea salad with preserved lemon; pork tenderloin with broccoli salad, cheddar gnocchi, bacon, and coffee agro dolce; and braised pork collar, rosemary creamed brussels sprouts, poached apple, toasted hazelnuts, and orange glaze.

Other choices include an exciting charcuterie board with cured meats, sausages, and pâtés, and house-made pickles; Ohio beef

Left: The cozy dining room at Black Pig in Ohio City.

Right: Thick bacon is topped with sugar and brûléed with a blowtorch at Black Pig.

tartare with harissa and pickled sunchokes; and a fettuccine Bolognese with Ohio lamb. Reasonably priced are a three-course tasting menu and a three-course pasta tasting menu, both with frequently changing dishes based on what is in season as well as the chef's whims. A talented pastry chef makes excellent desserts.

Creative cocktail choices include such exotic concoctions as the International Waters, made with Rhum JM Silver, Boulard calvados, grapefruit, lemon, Yunnan tea syrup, and a full measure of bitters. The bar includes an extensive wine list and craft beers.

2801 Bridge Ave.
216-862-7551
blackpigcle.com

LARDER DELICATESSEN AND BAKERY

A neighborhood deli and so much more

Inside a historic brick firehouse building, this "curated delicatessen" and bakery was new on the scene in 2018 but is already gaining national attention, and rightly so. Don't let the deli part fool you. This may be comfort food, but at the helm are three talented young chefs who honed their culinary skills at top restaurants before doing their own thing.

Clevelander Jeremy Umansky worked for Jonathon Sawyer, the James Beard Award-winning chef (see page 12). He and Sawyer really got into culturing koji, a fungus used in making soy sauce, sake, and miso paste. Umansky is also a pro in foraging and vinegar, and he helped Sawyer write his book *House of Vinegar*. Yes, he's a food whiz. Expect more fame to follow.

Umansky is married to baker Allie La Valle-Umansky, whom he met while attending the Culinary Institute of America. Their partner, Kenny Scott, graduated from Johnson & Wales University. The chefs use locally sourced and foraged ingredients in creations that are both familiar and elevated. Certified Angus Beef brisket is turned into pastrami in only a couple of days through the magic of koji and served thick cut on Allie's rustic rye. A perfectly flaky potato knish soars into the stratosphere with a topping of sour cream, golden

Fulfilling a goal to be a social community spot, Larder offers classes in fermenting (koji, sauerkraut), charcuterie, baking, and canning and preserving. Or join the chefs on a foraging expedition to such places as the Nelson-Kennedy Ledges State Park.

Left: Clevelander and koji expert Jeremy Umansky is one of a trio of talented chefs who created the updated deli. (Photo by Fran Golden)

Right: Larder's version of a fried chicken sandwich comes with pickled onions and a special sauce. (Photo by Nicole Steffen of @EatLocalOhio)

caviar, and fresh dill. If you see foraged mushrooms on the daily chalk board menu, go for it.

You order at the counter and may watch the chefs preparing your food. They'll also talk food if you want—Umansky, in particular, has a lot to say.

The décor includes photos and memorabilia as reminders that from 1854, and for 125 years, this was an Ohio City firehouse (Cleveland's Rising Star Coffee now occupies the other half of the building). The high ceilings allowed Larder room for soaring reclaimed cabinetry, the shelves stocked with jars of pickled things and vinegars. An old stove and oven were repurposed as a place for condiments and are where you deposit your tray after your meal.

Diners sit at a half-dozen tables and at picnic tables outside. You may do takeout, though it's a fun spot to linger and socialize, sipping the house-brewed root beer. Be sure to pick up rye bread, braided challah, or chocolate babka to bring home. You may grab a jar of jam, milk, and a selection of other grocery items from the larder while you're at it.

1455 W. 29th St.
216-912-8203
larderdb.com

MOMOCHO MOD MEX

Modern Mexican with an edge

Chef Eric Williams gets credit for popularizing Mexican food in Cleveland, although he admittedly does his own "Mod Mex" version at this hip Ohio City spot. His creative take includes six versions of creamy guacamole. When Guy Fieri stopped by for his Food Network show *Diners, Drive-ins and Dives*, he raved about "the guac gone wild," especially the house-smoked trout and bacon guacamole, though even the humbler goat cheese version is extremely satisfying. A sampler platter gets you several varieties, and all come with freshly fried house-made tortilla chips.

Also rave-worthy are the drinks, including five-dollar margaritas during the popular happy hour. For those who want to explore, there's an extensive list of dozens of tequilas and at least eight kinds of mezcal. The rest of the menu features tasty tamales and taquitos with surprising and often extravagant fillings, as well as heartier dishes, such as adobo lamb chops.

Mexican culture is celebrated in the playful décor, including scenes of lucha libre (Mexican pro wrestling) and Day of the Dead. Sit upstairs if you're looking for quieter dining and a glimpse of the kitchen, downstairs for a lively bar scene, or outdoors under umbrellas on the expansive patio.

Chef Eric Williams is also a partner with Chef Randy Carter in Jack Flaps Urban Breakfast Shoppe (3900 Lorain Ave., 216-961-5199, jackflaps.co), a small Ohio City café open for breakfast and lunch and serving such treats as buttermilk lemon curd pancakes, a house bacon of pork belly slow cooked with Mexican cola, and bourbon apple crisp waffles. In addition, he owns El Carnicero in Lakewood and is a partner in Happy Dog (see page 132).

Top left: Momocho Mod Mex is a lively restaurant with décor that includes references to Mexican pro wrestling.

Top right: On a summer night, the place to be is the spacious patio out back.

Above left: You can make a meal of small dishes such as the impressive variety of taquitos, or choose larger plate selections.

Above right: A Day of the Dead painting decorates a wall in the patio.

1835 Fulton Rd.
216-694-2122
momocho.com

SALT+

Creative small plates in a comfy neighborhood place

Chef Jill Vedaa in 2018 was a semifinalist for the James Beard Award for Best Chef: Great Lakes Region. The nomination was perhaps all the sweeter since she was nominated along with her mentor Chef Karen Small, whom she had worked for at Cleveland's Flying Fig (see page 128).

At her own lively brick-walled bistro opened in Lakewood in 2016, Vedaa and business partner Jessica parkison have created a hip venue where the focus is on shared plates and creative cocktails. You can sit at tables, the nice long bar, or seating areas with couches designed for conversation. Local musicians perform on Monday nights. The menu changes seasonally and is always full of surprises. Thoughtfully composed dishes embrace various global flavors.

You'll always find the popular white bean puree with mashed olives and grilled bread, usually a beet dish, and everyone's favorite—calamari with coriander coconut glaze and cilantro. Liver lovers will be thrilled with the chicken liver pâté with toasted rye and house-made pickles. If there's mussels in beer broth, that's a good choice too. From there Vedaa sets her creativity free, and you're never quite sure what delicious combinations she'll come up with. A featured dish might be pork tenderloin with pineapple salsa, mole glaze, and queso fresco. You might find something with radicchio or something with kimchi.

Servers are excellent and will make sure you order the right number of small plates for your table. The wine list has some unusual finds, and beers include rotating Ohio brewery drafts. Cocktails are designed to make you smile: the Jeff Spicoli—named

Left: Chef Jill Vedaa was nominated for a James Beard Award in 2018.

Right: The menu changes seasonally, every dish a creative treat. (Photos by Megann Galehouse for Salt+)

for a character in Fast Times at Ridgemont High—combines oven-roasted sweet corn–infused OYO rye (an Ohio product), sweet corn shrub, and brown sugar syrup, all of which is then applewood smoked.

Nearly all the restaurants in this book are in the city proper, but we made an exception for this favorite spot in Lakewood (right across the border).

While she didn't win the 2018 James Beard award, Vedaa did gain standing with Food Network fans as a winner of *Guy's Grocery Games*. When referring to the restaurant with your friends, keep in mind that the plus sign in the name is silent. Vedaa's flavors are enhanced with just a dash.

17625 Detroit Ave., Lakewood
216-221-4866
saltcleveland.com

WEST SIDE MARKET

City's #1 must-do foodie stop

Cleveland's big and beautiful, municipally owned covered food market opened in 1912 at the corner of 25th and Lorain in Ohio City. Listed on the National Register of Historic Places, it's still going strong. Dozens of vendors sell everything from soup to nuts, including fresh seafood, meats, and prepared food items. You might walk away with anything from bratwurst to soul food to a jug of fresh Ohio maple syrup.

As you peruse the aisles and the wares, you can reward yourself with treats—munching a crepe from Crêpes de Luxe or a chunk of spicy beef jerky from J & J Czuchraj Meats. An open-air market opened here in 1840, and the permanent yellow brick building, with iconic 137-foot clock tower, was designed by architects Benjamin Hubbell and W. Dominick Benes, who were responsible for other famous buildings in the city, including the Cleveland Museum of Art. Make sure to pull your eyes away from the food offerings long enough to look up at the forty-four-foot high Guastavino tile-vaulted ceiling.

If you're curious about how the market looked like in its earlier years, check out the historic images displayed above the vendor stands. The fruit and veggie vendors occupy an arcade portion that was enclosed and heated in 2004.

A million people visit each year. The market is open five days a week (closed Tuesdays, Thursdays).

1979 West 25th St.
216-664-3387
westsidemarket.org

Fruit and vegetable purveyors are in an arcade that was enclosed in 2004.

Favorites at the market:

The Cheese Shop

The glass cases of this cheese stand serve up some 175 imported and domestic temptations, but for locavores the draw is that this is the flagship retail outlet for Cleveland-based Lake Erie Creamery. Sample LEC's goat cheese (chévre), a cream cheese in several flavors. The staff are members of the American Cheese Society and know their stuff.

Crêpes de Luxe

The Parisian-style crepes are made with local ingredients, some gathered right at the market, and wrapped so that you can eat while you wander. A favorite is Le Chévre, with Lake Erie Creamery goat cheese, baby organic spinach, and tomato in a buckwheat crepe. Sweet crepes include the Classic, with banana, Nutella, and powdered sugar.

J & J Czuchraj Meats

Czuchraj (SHOO-cray) is a family-owned and-operated business started in 1954. They make smoked meats (kielbasa, smokies) and the best jerky you'll ever try. Chef Michael Symon helped put them on the map nationally (though locals knew the secret), mentioning their beef jerky in an episode of the Food Network's *The Best Thing I Ever Ate*. President Obama once stopped by. The meats are natural, hormone and preservative free, and smoked on hickory wood.

Mediterranean Imported Foods

This shop in a corner of the market was founded in 1969 by a Greek cheesemaker and offers an eye-popping selection of some three thousand Mediterranean and other gourmet products, including more types of feta cheese than you've likely ever seen in one place. Stock up on olive oil, coffee, cheese, and more.

Maha's Falafil

Maha's has been a West Side Market staple since 1986. The family-owned stand serves what is arguably the best falafel in town, as well as gyros, shawarmas, and fish dinners, all takeout. You can even get egg and falafel for breakfast or go with the Falafil Wrap Fully Loaded, with falafel, hummus, lettuce, tomato, pickled turnips, onion, fries, and tahini sauce in pita bread.

Ohio City Pasta

Ohio City Pasta is an institution in town—the go-to fresh artisan pasta maker not only for home cooks but also for some restaurants. No artificial ingredients and no flavor enhancements are used to make pasta in a great many varieties, with twenty flavors of ravioli alone.

Left: The market opened in 1912. Its 137-foot clock tower is a city icon.

Right: Many Cleveland area cooks start their Friday or Saturday mornings at the Market, planning and purchasing ingredients for a dinner party. Popular vendors include Ohio City Pasta. You may purchase pork for your sauce across the aisle.

TOWNHALL

A moss wall, no genetically modified organisms

Popcorn tofu nuggets, wild mushroom chimichangas, and cauliflower T-bone steak lead the Monday vegan nights at TownHall, one of the leaders in the hip Ohio City neighborhood's restaurant, bar, and nightlife scene. TownHall is not all vegan or vegetarian. A paleo menu, also known as the diet for caveman hunters and gatherers, is available on Wednesdays, but this thriving eatery draws a healthy crowd each evening at least partly because the menu is mostly organic and 100 percent non-GMO (no genetically modified organisms in the food).

One indoor wall is covered with moss, intended to invoke a sense of tranquility and peace while feeling closer to nature. The moss wall is said to improve the air quality and mindfulness of diners because living greenery absorbs CO_2 and removes harmful volatile organic compounds from the ambient air.

Owner Bobby George, who eats many of his meals at TownHall, says that he hired a consultant to screen everything that comes into his kitchen. "Either they've got to be verified by the Non-GMO Project or are Certified USDA Organic," he says in a mission paper. You'll find lots of quinoa and kale in a fun menu that includes slow-simmered bone broth; prosciutto-wrapped dates; paella of wild shrimp, chorizo, sweet peas, provolone, and saffron aioli; and Asian-inspired bowls and flatbreads. The coffee is organic and independently lab tested to ensure it is free of all molds and mycotoxins. Juices, all made in-house and cold-pressed, are organic, and the smoothie bar includes Chinese berries.

This eatery is not swanky; it's more like a beer garden, especially in good weather, when the crowd spreads to patios in front and in back. TownHall has become a gathering spot for local professional athletes and celebrities, including Khloé Kardashian, who in 2018

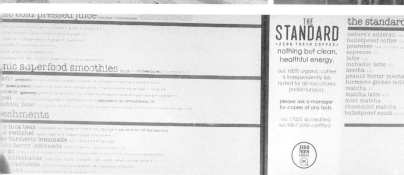

Top left: In warm weather, the TownHall crowd spills outside in front and back, giving the popular restaurant a beer hall feel.

Top right: Tables sit high, and many are communal. Menus are on the walls.

Above: Food and drink choices mostly are organic and are 100 percent non-GMO.

was spotted and displayed on a video obtained by TMZ. She was lunching with the father of her child, Tristan Thompson, an NBA basketball player for the Cleveland Cavaliers. Both were wearing black outfits.

1909 W. 25th St.
216-344-9400
townhallohiocity.com

JOHNNY MANGO WORLD CAFE & BAR

Hipster hangout, daily selection of meatless happy beans

The cuisine is Mexico and Jamaica meets Asian, and many among the patrons and bar staff are hipsters with tattoos. When it opened in 1996, Johnny Mango was one of the first places in the Ohio City neighborhood with a good selection of vegetarian and vegan, as the original owner, Shelley Underwood, wanted to focus on healthy eating. The restaurant's name was chosen because it sounds like a fictional world traveler.

New owners in 2018 are Underwood's sister, Mandy Kiczek, and chef JT Haynes, who started working at Johnny Mango as a dishwasher. The décor is casual, friendly, even beachy. Artwork and a maze of greenery adorn the walls and shelves. Dishes are tasty and flavorful. Pad thai, Bangkok BBQ chicken, and black bean quesadilla get well-deserved raves. Be ready for the fieriness of the Jamaican jerk chicken. Look for discounts on tacos during Taco Tuesdays. Every month gets a theme—January is Hot Soup Month, July is salad, May is margaritas. The menu includes a different meatless "happy beans" presentation each day. Vegan nachos come with house-made vegan cheese sauce.

At the juice bar, you can go savory or sweet. Juices and margaritas (from the full-service bar) are sold by the glass or pitcher. The Morning After—tomato, carrot, celery, scallions, green peppers, and garlic—is said to cure what ails you.

3120 Bridge Ave.
216-575-1919
jmango.com

Top right: It's always a beachy day at Johnny Mango, with brightly painted walls, colorful flowers, and a casual attitude.

Top left: The full-service bar can go savory or sweet. The juice bar is legendary, and margaritas are sold by the glass or pitcher.

Above left: Cleveland summers seem short, and so are some restaurant patios.

Above right: Fulton Road and Bridge Avenue meet like a slice of pie, which explains the shape of the Johnny Mango building.

THE HARP IRISH PUB AND RESTAURANT

For soda bread, boxty cakes, and colcannon

With traditional and contemporary Irish food and a long list of Irish labels behind the bar, the Harp is one of the finest Irish pubs in the United States and has a list of reviews to prove it.

The warm, bustling, melodious Harp restaurant is busy every day with locals as well as travelers looking for a taste of Ireland. Inside or outdoors on a patio overlooking Lake Erie you will find fresh-baked soda bread, shepherd's pie, Irish whiskey mustard chicken over colcannon (mashed potatoes with kale or cabbage), and boxty cakes, an Irish potato pancake folded and stuffed with such items as corned beef, sauerkraut, Swiss cheese, and Russian dressing.

Owner Karen O'Malley wanted Cleveland to have an Irish pub like the ones in her father's old home village of Achill Island in County Mayo, where all the pubs overlooked water. Michael O'Malley looked for a spot of land on the bluffs along the shore near downtown. That was not easy, as Cleveland was built for industry and Great Lakes shipping. O'Malley bought a car wash with a sweeping view of Lake Erie and replaced it with a restaurant.

Irish music fills the air (live band weekly), surrounded by carved wood walls, stained glass, murals created by Irish artisans, a fireplace, and a wooden bar designed in Ireland.

4408 Detroit Ave.
216-939-0200
the-harp.com

154

Top left: A quiet lunch spot at The Harp, with a view of Lake Erie.

Top right: In a lineup of beers on tap at The Harp, the first two pulls are Guinness, an Irish dry stout that originated in the brewery of Arthur Guinness in Dublin, Ireland, in 1759.

Above left: Road signs at The Harp in Cleveland bring a smile but little in the way of geographical assistance.

Above right: Jameson is the mostly popular Irish Whiskey in the world.

JOHNNY'S BAR ON FULTON

Northern Italian food and nymphs on the walls

Normally, you should beware of the food in a restaurant with a big sign outside that shouts "BAR," especially if there's no mention of the restaurant. But don't worry about the sign or the food at Johnny's Bar, a Cleveland classic serving fine Northern Italian cuisine. The restaurant has two rooms with a Rat Pack vibe, a considerable buzz, tightly packed tables with white tablecloths, a single rose on each table, and murals with nymphs on the walls. Frank Sinatra might have eaten here, and he would feel at home with a drink at the bar. You might hum a few Sinatra songs when the evening's musician takes a break.

The building has housed a restaurant in this old blue-collar neighborhood for nearly a hundred years, opening in the 1920s as Louise's Garden, and flourishing as Johnny's on Fulton, about ten minutes from downtown, since 1952. After you grab a snapshot of the ladies in the murals, put your phone away. Cell phones are banned (it's written on the menu).

Johnny's is known for serving fancy, well-designed appetizers and carefully plated main courses. Try peppercorn-crusted duck breast, stuffed calamari, burrata, chopped kale salad, seafood stew in rich marinara sauce, or the popular steak au poivre. The list of Italian red wines is extensive, particularly Tuscan and Piedmontese, with beers on tap. Patio seating is out back. Owner Bo Santosuosso borrowed the recipes, style, and name, Johnny's, for his highly rated restaurant Johnny's Downtown. (see page 22)

3164 Fulton Rd.
216-281-0055
johnnysonfulton.com

Top: Mythical figures guard the walls on a mural inside Johnny's.

Above left: Though food is not mentioned on the sign outside on Fulton Road, the eatery is implied, and it is well worth walking in the door.

Above right: Veal-stuffed banana peppers with Asiago cheese and marinara sauce are a specialty of the house.

BRUNO'S RISTORANTE

Friendly Italian classics in football player portions

In 1996, Cleveland lost its beloved NFL professional football team, the Browns, which moved to Baltimore (a new team with the old name but without its skills was reborn in 1999). Cleveland's loss was also Cleveland's gain, as Bruno DiSiena, the football team's chef and caterer, stayed in town to establish his own Italian restaurant. Dishes at Bruno's Ristorante, heavy on the red sauce, arrive in portions big enough to feed football players or the rest of us who come to take some food home for lunch the next day.

Bruno's occupies the front rooms of a street corner home in a residential neighborhood near the city's old Stockyards on the near West Side. There's nothing impressive about the building, though the restaurant has added a spacious patio with tables, plants, and umbrellas for good weather. Inside, the décor includes landscape prints of Coreno, Italy, the owners' old family hometown in the hills southeast of Rome. A full wooden bar includes Italian regional wines, Italian beers, and an espresso machine. White cloths cover the tables in a setting so intimate that you may hear a few family conversations from tables nearby, as Bruno's has become a casual hangout for neighborhood friends, family, and occasionally former Browns football players.

The waitstaff is friendly, and the menu is mostly pizza, homemade pasta, and Italian dinner entrées. The antipasti plate is filled with a generous portion of meats, Fontina cheese, roasted peppers, and olives. Other items include calamari fritti, chicken cacciatore, vitello alla parmigiana (veal with provolone), linguine alla pescatore (seafood sautéed in a light marinara sauce), and lasagna, voted best in Cleveland in a magazine poll. Desserts are homemade. Tiramisu,

Left: Bruno's occupies a street-corner house, fronting on one-way, north-bound W. 41st Street. You may need to use your GPS to find it in the city's old stockyards neighborhood.

Top right: Bruno's intimate dining room occupies the front of the house.

Above right: A full wooden bar includes Italian regional wines, Italian beers, and a big espresso machine.

the signature dessert, is from a recipe of the owner's mother. Make a reservation, especially on weekends.

Many of the regulars at lunch hand over their car keys at the car wash across the across the street. It's owned by the brother of executive chef Bruno DiSiena, and he will wash while you eat.

2644 W. 41st St.
216-961-7087
brunosristorante.net

BANTER

Poutine gets a hip, Cleveland-style remake

A brick building in the Gordon Square Arts District houses this quirky offering of casual dining in a beer and wine store. The sign outside tells the story: "Bottles, Sausage, Poutine." The place was opened in 2015 by locals Matthew Stipe, Adam Gullett, and Tom Owen, who had been coworkers at other restaurants. You head to the counter to order from the short menu posted on retro black letterboards, and your meal comes on metal trays.

Poutine, the decadent dish of French fries, cheese curd, and gravy, is featured, and Banter's version is insane. Thick-cut fries are topped with sauces that include rabbit pot pie and chicken paprikash (with smoked chicken, spaetzli, curds, and crème fraîche). The Vladamir Poutine (get it?) is braised Ohio lamb stroganov, curds, and gravy. Banter gets its proteins from Ohio City Provisions, meaning all the meat is Ohio raised.

Sausage is the star of sandwiches, including a traditional Polish Boy, with house-made BBQ sauce and coleslaw. The Clevelander packs together a bunch of local tastes, including kielbasa and a pierogi, sauerkraut, and Bertman Original mustard. Or try something new, such as the yummy fried chicken sausage. There are sliders on the menu, too.

Accompany your meal with pours from the ten international and local craft beers on tap, choose wine by the glass, or head to backrooms and explore the hundreds of bottles of wine and more than four hundred beer and cider options.

7320 Detroit Ave.
216-801-0305
bantercleveland.com

Top left: The hipster spot is upfront about its proposition. (BrukleHagen Photography)

Top right: Even the furniture is cool at Banter. (BrukleHagen Photography)

Middle left: Whether you come to eat, drink, or both, open your mind to indulgence. (Peter Larson Photography)

Above left: Poutine in many forms is the menu highlight. (Peter Larson Photography)

Above right: Order wine by the glass or head to the backrooms to choose from hundreds of bottles. (BrukleHagen Photography)

CORNER 11 BOWL & WRAP

Friendly neighborhood spot for poke, Northern Thai

Hawaiian-style poke (pronounced poh-keh) is a recent addition to the Cleveland food scene. The best spot to try the dish of raw tuna (or your choice of another protein) on a bowl of rice, with all sorts of wonderful toppings, is this friendly little neighborhood spot in the Tremont neighborhood. Thiwaporn Sirisuwan and her husband, Sam, opened this counter-service place on a corner across from Lincoln Park in 2017. They came from Thailand so that he could attend law school at Case Western Reserve University. In Bangkok, she earned a master's degree in advertising. When they realized that Cleveland did not have a stand-alone poke spot, they decided to do something about that.

In researching their menu, Thiwaporn and Sam traveled to Hawaii and California. For the bowls, which they offer in three sizes, you select a base of white rice, vitamin-packed midnight rice (imported from Thailand) or salad greens, and a protein. In addition to sushi-grade tuna and salmon, such options as cooked shrimp, scallops, chicken, and tofu are available. Then you choose from a colorful array of additional toppings displayed in a glass case—everything from edamame and seaweed salad to tomatoes and avocado. There's even caviar! You can go crazy creating your own bowl. The several sauce options include some sweet and mildly spicy choices.

> Thiwaporn Sirisuwan says she and Sam discovered poke while traveling. "We like to travel, and we love food. When we travel around the U.S., there are so many cultures, different people," she says.

Left: Create your own poke bowl, choosing from dozens of fresh ingredients.
Middle: The friendly cafe is located across the street from Tremont's Lincoln Park.
Right: The menu also features ramen and other hot dishes.

Doing takeout is a popular option though. With windows on the park, high tops and tables with views, outdoor picnic tables, and even a porch-like living room area, this is also a comfy, homey place to linger.

The poke is delicious, but don't let that option distract you from the rest of the menu that includes dishes from Thiwaporn's native Chiang Rai in Northern Thailand. Some are based on family recipes. Some, such as the sai oua, a mild sausage, are actually made by her mother when she comes from Thailand to visit (they sometimes run out of the sausage in between mom's visits).

Thiwaporn's cousin cooks at a Thai restaurant in Los Angeles and shared the recipe for the yen ta fo (pink noodle soup). A creamy yellow curry noodle soup is an option. The "wrap" part of the menu is wonton soup, spring rolls, ka nom jeeb (Thai dumplings), and steamed buns. Fussier eaters will be happy with the beef or chicken teriyaki.

2391 W. 11th St.
216-713-1757
corner11cleveland.com

Clevelanders love their donuts, even with beer

The city has seen increased competition in the realm of everyone's favorite fried treat—donuts. Getting local and national attention for good reason is Brewnuts, serving donuts that are both made with and paired with craft beer. The motto of the colorful shop, owned by two Clevelanders, Shelley and John Pippen, is "Donut Mess with Cleveland." They started their concept at the Cleveland Flea, a popular outdoor summertime flea market, and grew from there.

In the batter, alcohol burns off in the cooking process, and the result is a nice fluffy donut. For those who want more, beer sometimes makes appearances at Brewnuts in icing, filling, or topping. Sample chocolate donuts made with stout or maple bacon made with Tree Tapper Maple Brown beer. Options change frequently.

All the donuts are made by hand and sold until they run out (don't get there too late in the day). On Sundays, you may find a savory option, such as a fried mac & cheese donut. On the beer side, sixteen local brews are on tap as well as cans and bottles. Phoenix Coffee is brewed for those seeking a more traditional pairing.

Well-known baker Courtney Bonning does her artisanal donut thing at Bigmouth Donut Company in the Hingetown neighborhood, where everything is from scratch. Even the frostings and fillings are made in-house. The name was chosen because it's easy to remember even after you've had a few drinks, says co-owner Kelly Brewer.

Bigmouth's classic yeast donuts include the popular vanilla bean-glazed and premium yeast donuts that come in more than a dozen flavors, including apple chai frosted, Ohio Buckeye, and key lime coconut. Try cake donuts and apple fritters or egg and cheese on

Left: At Brewnuts, donuts made with, and served with, beer are the attraction.

Right: Maybe they tossed down a few donuts and some brews before they made the sign.

a donut (you may add sausage or bacon). Phoenix Coffee is the preferred accompaniment. Check out the mural by award-winning local artist George Kocar.

For a crazy big variety of more traditional donuts, head to the Old Brooklyn neighborhood and the award-winning Jack Frost, family owned and operated since 1937. Choose from more than two hundred types of yeast-raised and cake donuts and crullers, apple fritters, and cinnamon rolls made from scratch each night. Favorites include honey-glazed, maple-iced (with or without bacon), and Death by Chocolate—a raised donut with chocolate icing, chocolate custard, chocolate syrup drizzle, chocolate cream, and brown sprinkles with a chocolate hazelnut pirouette stick. Some of the donuts have huge amounts of frosting, and some get crowd-pleasing toppings, such as Fruity Pebbles, Reese's Puffs, and Apple Jacks.

Brewnuts
6501 Detroit Rd.
216-600-9579
brewnutscleveland.com

Bigmouth Donuts
1418 W. 29th St.
216-282-8228
bigmouthdonut.com

Jack Frost Donuts
4960 Pearl Rd.
216-351-3638
jackfrostdonutsusa.com

EL RINCONCITO CHAPIN

Guatemalan flavors in a casual neighborhood spot

This affordable Old Brooklyn neighborhood café focuses its menu on authentic Guatemalan cuisine, with its Mayan and Spanish influences. Owner Engel Godinez is a Guatemala native who moved to Cleveland to cook, which he did at restaurants in and around the city before deciding to introduce Clevelanders to his native cuisine. He moved into this bright little stand-alone building, which was once an Arby's, in 2018. The name of the restaurant roughly translates as "little Guatemalan corner."

You can eat in with table service at one of the booths or order takeout at the counter, where helpful photos show you what to expect. Prices are affordable. Most entrées are under fifteen dollars. Generous servings of house specialties include a carne asada dinner (grilled skirt steak with refried black beans, rice, guacamole, and salsa) served with tortillas and a take on the classic stewed chicken dish called pepián, here with red pepper sauce.

For a variety of tastes, you can also order up popular Guatemalan street foods, for example, a Chapin Sampler gets you several, including Guatemalan-style tamales and mini bean and cheese pupusas. Don't miss the garnachas, which are six fried mini tortillas topped with shredded beef, onion, salsa, cilantro and queso fresco.

3330 Broadview Rd. (Old Brooklyn)
216-795-5776
facebook.com/elrinconcitochapinCLE

Left: A bottle of Guatemalan hot sauce is on every table.

Top middle: Owner and Chef Engel Godinez came from Guatemala to work at Cleveland-area restaurants, before opening his own spot.

Top right: The restaurant occupies a former Arby's.

Above right: Among must-try dishes is the flavorful guarachas.

Authentic Ethiopian in the heart of the city

Taytu Betul, Empress of the Ethiopian Empire at the end of the nineteenth century, was one of the most formidable females in Ethiopian history. She started the Ethiopian Red Cross, founded the capital of Addis Ababa, and single-handedly led the Ethiopian army to victory over nine hundred Italian troops at the Siege of Mek'ele in 1896. She also ruled the country on her own when her husband, Emperor Menalik II, fell ill.

When Carl and Senait Robson decided to open an Ethiopian restaurant in Cleveland in 1992, Robson remembers saying, "We have to call it Empress Taytu!" Decades later, Empress Taytu in Cleveland's St. Clair–Superior neighborhood continues to draw diners from all parts of the city, who come as much for the experience as the meal.

With tiny sparkling lights hanging from the ceiling, walls covered with photographs of Robson's Ethiopian travels, and traditional mesobs (low rattan tables) throughout the restaurant, patrons will feel as if they've hopped a flight to Gonder when they enter Empress Taytu. The menu offers authentic Ethiopian dishes, such as the spicy doro wat chicken stew and lamb tips, a ginger and garlic-seasoned lamb stir fry, which diners eat with injera—a sponge-like flatbread—as well as plenty of vegetarian options.

> "It was a couple of years after the Hough Riots [in 1966] when we opened. You'd see black nationalists on the corner. There were Muslim bakeries along St. Clair. It was peaceable."
> –Owner, Carl Robson

Left: Be transported to Ethiopia, if just for a meal, at Empress Taytu.

Right: Sample avocado salad, chicken and beef tibs (cubes), and injera (flatbread), accompanied by a Xingu black beer. (Photos courtesy of Empress Taytu)

To be truly transported, order the ritual Ethiopian coffee ceremony after your meal. The leisurely ceremony begins with roasting Ethiopian coffee beans in the kitchen. Your server then brings the smoking pan of aromatic beans to your table and pours the coffee from a jebena (clay pot) into sinis (small traditional coffee cups), while frankincense is burned at your table. The coffee is served with sugar but no milk and accompanied by ambasha, a pan-cooked Ethiopian bread. The ritual is an integral part of the cultural life in Ethiopia and considered a mark of friendship.

Service at Empress Taytu is gracious and friendly, and most of the staff are Ethiopian, including owner Senait Robson. A former flight attendant for Ethiopian Airlines, she met her husband, Carl, a doctor, when she came to Cleveland to study nursing. She is part of a small but close-knit Ethiopian community in Cleveland, for which Empress Taytu has become a popular gathering place.

6125 St. Clair Ave.
216-391-9400
empresstayturestaurantcleveland.com

FARKAS PASTRY SHOPPE

Hungarian pastry made from old-world recipes

It's rare to find real krémes outside of Budapest, but Sandor Farkas, a Hungarian master pastry chef, came to Cleveland in the 1960s armed with old-world recipes, and more than fifty years later the shop he started still sells the delicious layers of custard and whipped cream between paper thin layers of puff pastry, dusted with powdered sugar—think the Hungarian equivalent to French napoleons.

Stop by the friendly shop open Wednesdays to Sundays and you may think you're back in the old country—customers speaking several different languages line up not only for the krémes but also for linzer tortes filled with apples, raspberry/hazelnut, or pineapple/walnut; whole dobos tortes (six layers of crispy sponge cake layered with buttercream and topped with marzipan); and nut rolls. Options also include the gluten-free, five-layer Esterházy torte, named for the nineteenth century Hungarian prince, and made with baked almond meringue holding together layers of real buttercream and apricot filling, all topped with fondant.

For those who prefer savory, try the traditional terpertős pogácsa, flaky scone-like biscuits flavored with pork cracklings. Bring the handmade treats to a party and you'll be the superstar.

2700 Lorain Ave.
216-281-6200
farkaspastries.com

Top: The bakery has been a fixture in Cleveland for more than 50 years.

Right: Sample decadent treats made from Old World recipes. (Photos courtesy of Farkas Pastry Shoppe)

Fresh croissant and coffee in University Circle

Croissant master Ben Woods helms this bakery café in the University Circle area (near the main campus of Cleveland Clinic). The menu includes farm-to-table salads, pizzas, sandwiches, and breakfast items, but the real wow is in the croissants, pastries, and scones, baked fresh daily and made with a deft hand—the perfect accompaniment to the handcrafted coffee drinks. While you're there, you'll want to take away a loaf or two of Woods' artisan breads (especially the sourdough).

Fluffy Duck is all about organic products. Meats are pasture raised and hormone free (and come from Ohio City Provisions, an all-local butcher), produce comes from farms located within seventy-five miles of Cleveland, and salads are made from greens hydroponically grown in Cleveland.

Woods is a graduate of the Culinary Institute of America and worked in kitchens in Georgia; Portland, Oregon; and England before coming home to Cleveland to open his own café on the first floor of a luxury apartment building. Thanks to the open kitchen, patrons can watch the baking process while making choices from the glass cases. The coffee drinks are made on a fancy La Marzocco espresso machine, and the coffee beans are Madcap, imported from Grand Rapids, Michigan.

10001 Chester Ave.
216-218-9447
fluffyduckcafe.com

Left: Fresh-baked croissants and handcrafted coffee drinks are among the specialties at Fluffy Duck.

Right: Many of the organic ingredients are local, the coffee beans imported from nearby Michigan. (Photos courtesy of Fluffy Duck)

CHARLIE'S DOG HOUSE DINER

Old dog has a story, more bark than bite

Sometimes a tour bus pulls up outside this roadside shack on a busy commercial street southwest of downtown, and the nineteen counter seats and two at a tiny table fill quickly. On most days, however, even at the rushiest of rush hours, you will find an empty stool. Watch owner and cook Bobbi Malek prepare your meal at a grill so close that you can judge the runniness of your egg yolks before you cut into them and then be on your way in short order.

Cleveland's kitschy version of the Dog House Diner has been going strong since 1952. It was originally part of a national chain of shops started during the Great Depression to sell cheap food, particularly hot dogs. The diners were manufactured in Wichita, Kansas, by Valentine Manufacturing, Inc., from the late 1930s into the mid-1970s. Sales expanded nationwide and at one time numbered about 2,200 dog houses in a wide range of sizes. Some of those Valentine buildings are still in use today, but many serve other types of businesses, such as used car lot offices and dog grooming salons. One eight-stool Valentine building in Albuquerque, New Mexico, was converted into a police substation.

Photos of the old Dog House Diners are a tourist favorite. Cleveland's diner, which burned and required a rebuild, is more of a shack than anything else. Two lively dog pictures (Salt and Pepper) give the façade at the front a unique look, although Charlie's Dog House Diner is more than a cute place—it's a hardworking eatery that is worth a stop if you are hungry for malted waffles, eggs with hash browns or fries, hot dogs and chili dogs, burritos, corned beef hash, biscuits and gravy, skillet specials, or a country fried steak—all

Top left: Painted dogs, Salt and Pepper, greet patrons at Cleveland's version of the Dog House

Top right: Big Jim sat here for his early morning breakfasts.

Left: Counter and kitchen are close at Charlie's.

served with retro napkin holders and ketchup on the counter. It's a fun spot to hang around with a cup of coffee and listen to the banter among the regulars.

You may read about the stool seat saved for Big Jim, marked with his name on the counter reserved for his early breakfast, starting at about 6:00 a.m. Don't worry about moving over should Big Jim arrive to claim his seat. Like many of those old Valentine Dog Diner buildings, Big Jim has passed away.

2102 Brookpark Rd.
216-661-4873
facebook.com/Charlies-Dog-House-Diner-118250088187413

Where the recipes and the restaurant are one hundred years old

A century ago, Vincenzo Guarino left his native Sicily to seek his fortune in America and decided to live in a newly settled Italian neighborhood in Cleveland. Surprise: it was on a hill. Guarino opened a pool hall in a neighborhood that soon became known as Little Italy. When he married a local girl, she suggested that food be served. They were successful, using her family recipes for lasagna, veal, and braciola to lure a mixture of the city's East Siders, both secretive local brigands of the times as well as professors and musicians from the nearby cultural and educational institutions. During prohibition, Guarino served liquor in coffee cups, while his mother-in-law had a thriving wine business on the next street.

The family lived upstairs in an apartment that in the 1950s became an elegant townhouse with three generations of Guarinos. Family and friends still manage, cook, and serve Mama Mary Guarino's recipes. Today, nothing appears modern, but the patrons seem to like things that way at Cleveland's oldest restaurant, since 1918. It gets raves for lasagna and eggplant parm. Specialties include Italian wedding soup, chicken piccata, and frutti di mare (seafood and pasta), veal saltimbocca and braciola, which is rolled steak stuffed with prosciutto, onions, provolone, and raisins served over pasta. You can get a classic Manhattan or a Capone (bourbon and Campari).

The restaurant has a neon sign out front and a retro vibe inside, which is done up in Victorian décor, with guests dining in parlors. On the patio out back is statuary, fountains, string lights, and a garden opened in 1959 that still holds trumpet vines and grape vines that Vincenzo Guarino brought from Sicily.

Top left: You never know what piece of history you might spot while eating at Guarino's, now 100 years old.

Right: The first family Guarino lived above the restaurant, and all worked downstairs.

Above left: Like most of the other older restaurants in Little Italy, Guarino's is on Mayfield Road, on the hill climbing from Univerisity Circle toward the suburbs in the Heights. Unlike most of the others, Guarino's has its own parking lot.

12309 Mayfield Rd.
216-231-3100
guarinoscleveland.com

LA PLAZA SUPERMARKET AND TAQUERIA

Real Mexican tacos at a supermarket in Cleveland

Forget the ambience. This supermarket operated by the Ortega family and located at the Cleveland-Lakewood border serves the best, most authentic tacos in town. It's a secret that lots of people have discovered. The Mexican fare is so popular that the market in fall 2018 moved its taco stand from the back of the store, where you often had to wait in lines with dozens of other fans, to its own space out front, including seating for a few dozen guests. That's a good thing.

We're talking soft corn tacos, double or triple layered for easy handling and filled with tender steak asado and marinated pork or chicken. Add your own lime, cilantro, avocado crema, pico de gallo, or chili sauces. Everything—burritos and tostados are also available—is served in paper or take-out Styrofoam. Spend ten dollars and you'll be stuffed.

While you're there, don't ignore the rest of the store, where you'll find an impressive array of Latin goods, including dozens of types of dried chilies, elote fresco (cactus), plaintains, tomatillos, Mexican cola, and queso fresco. The friendly staff is around to help even if sometimes in a combination of Spanish and English. If you've got a sweet tooth, try the Mexican ice cream or splurge on tres leches cake.

13609 Lakewood Heights Blvd.
216-476-8000
laplazataqueria.com

Top left: Home cooks will find a wealth of Latin goods, including produce, at the supermarket.

Top right: Soft corn tortillas are double or triple layered to handle the delicious fillings inside.

Middle left: The taco stand, upgraded in 2018, is in the front of the supermarket.

Middle right: If you can't find the ingredient you are looking for, a friendly staff is there to help.

Above left: Word has gotten out about the great tacos, and you may have to wait in line if you arrive for lunch.

Above right: Looking for a particular kind of chili? Chances are La Plaza will have it.

LUCHITA'S MEXICAN RESTAURANT

Simple, decades old, family run

Opened in 1982 by Maria de la Luz Galindo Muñoz (Luchita) and her son Jorge Galindo, Luchita's was one of the city's original Mexican restaurants. Luchita herself worked in the kitchen until she was eighty-seven years old, passing away in 2016. Luchita's recipes still form a major portion of the menu, and some staff members have worked there for decades. Today, the eatery shows up in international dining guides, but it remains as it began: a simple, low-key, neighborhood, family-run business and a friendly corner bar.

Though early on they substituted vegetable oil for lard, the Galindo family continues to cook traditional Mexican sauces, such as mole, and the menu explains what goes into each dish. The signature item is tinga de pollo: shredded chicken, chorizo, chipotle salsa, queso panela, avocado, and sour cream. Regular diners are aware of special times for discounts (check the website), such as the after 4:00 p.m. price on Tuesdays for tacos at $1.50 and Wednesdays for enchiladas at $2.50.

The 1930s building is in a working-class neighborhood. Stucco walls are decorated with Mexican ceramics, figurines, and artwork.

3456 W. 117th St.
216-252-1169
luchitas.net

Top left: The restaurant is less than one mile south of the Interstate 90 exit at W. 117th Street.

Top right: Luchita's remains as it began: a simple, low-key, family-run business.

Above left: The bar is a neighborhood favorite.

Above right: Regular diners are aware of special times for discounts (check the website), such as the after 4:00 p.m. price on Tuesdays for tacos at $1.50 and Wednesdays for enchiladas at $2.50.

MITCHELL'S ICE CREAM

We all scream for ice cream

Ice cream is very much part of the local food scene despite the long winters. The brand everyone knows is Mitchell's, with nine locations in and around the city and available at local grocery stores. The flagship Mitchell's shop and production facility in Ohio City occupies a refurbished 1919 vaudeville theater, with marquee out front. It's an amazing space with lights, freezers, and refrigerators powered by solar panels. Furniture is made of recycled materials. Behind the counter you can watch the ice cream-making process through glass.

Co-owned by Clevelanders Mike and Pete Mitchell, the company has been in business for two decades and focuses on handcrafted ice cream (and vegan, sorbet, and yogurt selections) using local organic and fair trade certified ingredients. Caramel fudge brownie is one of the most popular flavors. Get your scoops on a freshly baked waffle cone.

Distinctive for the way it sweetens its ice cream is Honey Hut, a seasonal family business in Old Brooklyn that's been producing creamy homemade ice cream made with local Amish honey and Ohio milk since 1974. Korean vet and active duty firefighter Frank Page was the founder, and before introducing new flavors, he sometimes tested them on the firehouse crew at Ladder 42. Longtime favorites include honey pecan made with salted, locally sourced pecans and orange blossom, made with orange zest and orange blossom honey.

Sweet Moses in the Gordon Square Arts District is a perfectly designed retro 1950s malt shop. You can sit on a stool or at a table and order an excellent hot fudge sundae or fountain drink made at an authentic Bastion-Blessings soda fountain. The name of the place honors Moses Cleaveland, founder of the city. The hot fudge and

Left: With nine locations in and around Cleveland, Mitchell's Ice Cream is a local favorite.

Right: Mitchell's caramel fudge brownie is a particular crowd pleaser. (Photos courtesy of Mitchell's Ice Cream)

caramel sauces are made in-house; the ice cream is homemade and includes a whole vegan menu. They have their own Sweet Moses Root Beer and also sell other treats, such as homemade fudge.

Mason's Creamery, a small artisan shop in Ohio City, opened in 2013 by Northeast Ohio native Jesse Mason and Helen Qin from China, both who moved here from Los Angeles. They serve up small-batch homemade ice cream in classic, seasonal, and vegan flavors. Local ingredients, such as Rising Star Coffee and Cleveland Whiskey, make appearances. Creative takes include vanilla ice cream made with Ugandan vanilla and topped with sweet siracha. Seasonal offerings, such as pumpkin and Christmas eggnog, are popular choices. In winter, Mason's doubles as a ramen shop.

Mitchell's Ice Cream (flagship)
1867 W. 25th St.
216-861-2799
mitchellshomemade.com

Honey Hut
4674 State Rd.
216-749-7077
honeyhut.com

Mitchell's Ice Cream Uptown
(University Circle)
11444 Uptown Ave.
216-229-9402
mitchellshomemade.com

Sweet Moses
6800 Detroit Ave.
216-651-2202
sweetmosestreats.com

Mason's Creamery
4401 Bridge Ave.
216-762-1095

NATE'S DELI

Hummus, falafel, in a casual family-owned spot

Just down the street from the West Side Market and using fresh ingredients from the market is this small, family-owned Lebanese café that has been serving great hummus and falafel since the 1980s. The creamy and flavorful hummus at this unassuming spot gets well-deserved raves—made here with chickpeas, tahini, and lemon topped with olive oil, parsley, and paprika. There is great argument as to whether or not Nate's also makes the best falafel in town; some argue for Nate's, while others insist it's Maha's at the Market.

The menu also has homemade soups and deli sandwiches, but the real reason to come here is the well-prepared Middle Eastern fare. Shish kebab, shish tawook (marinated chicken on skewers), and kafta (seasoned beef patties) are all featured, or get a platter with all the selections. Nate's does a big takeout business, but you can also dine in at one of the few booths or tables.

1923 W. 25th St.
216-696-7529
natesohiocity.com

Nate's Deli & Restaurant

MEDITERRANEAN CUISINE

• IN CLEVELAND'S OHIO CITY •

Top: Tables are tight, but not crowded for a mid-afternoon deli lunch.

Above: The small family-owned Lebanese café has been serving great hummus and falafel since the 1980s.

THE PLUM

Creativity with a local edge

Walk into this hip but laid-back spot in the Lorain Historical District and you'll notice a Harlem Globetrotters classic pinball machine up against a brick wall in the corner. It's the first indication that the folks in the kitchen here like to play, including with ingredients. Chef Brett Sawyer believes eating should be an adventure. His menu of shared small and large plates is designed to expand the taste buds, adding a "wow" factor. The New American fare is served at contemporary high tops and tables in a room done up with bright floral wallpaper, and in a wonderful outdoor patio.

While the white-tiled bar is inviting as a spot for dining alone, coming with friends allows for sampling more dishes on the frequently changing seasonal menu, including the daily specials created with what is available at the market that day. Sawyer works with vendors, including Fallen Apple Farm in Ashland, Rittman Orchards in Doylestown, Red Basket Farm in Kinsman, Ohio City Farm, and the North Union Farmers Market. The philosophy is product first and then go from there.

The crowd is young and trendy, but older foodies will feel at home too. The best thing to bring is an open mind and a willingness to sample new flavors and combinations. Think a real-life version of the Food Network TV show *Chopped*, with dishes that are well composed and often daring. You might find, for instance, a whole fried General Tso's chicken served with miso peanut slaw and

Special menus celebrate holidays, including Mother's Day and Valentine's Day, while an amazing Sunday Supper Series brings other chefs from the Midwest in for creative playtime, and you get to eat the results in a meal served family style.

186

Left: Chef Brett Sawyer believes eating should be an adventure. (Photo by Berkel Hagen Studio)

Middle top: Sawyer elevates nibbles to new dimensions. (Photo by Mia L. Sultis)

Middle bottom: The dishes are big on "wow" factor. What appears simple often is quite complex. (Photo by Mia L. Sultis)

Right: Indulge in a sampling of large and small plates. (Photo by Mia L. Sultis)

pickled carrots or fried rice with the added ingredient of foie gras. Chips and dip may be in the form of mushroom puffs with pickled ramp dip.

The popular Snack Time menu includes Ma's pastelillos (the Puerto Rican street food staple), lamb burgers, and fried chicken sandwiches. Accompany your eats with wine selections or interesting drink combos, such as Sweet Reverie, made with vodka from Watershed Distillery (in Columbus, Ohio), hibiscus, lemon, honey, and Peychaud's bitters.

4133 Lorain Ave.
216-938-8711
theplumcafeandkitchen.com

Here's how Chef Brett Sawyer describes his cooking style: "All over the place. Nonconformist American." He wants the dining experience at The Plum to be "casual, tasty, and fun."

Authentic Puerto Rican dishes, including mofongo

This bright and lively little café in the Gordon Square Arts District serves authentic Puerto Rican cuisine made from scratch. The Ruiz family opened the casual spot in 2006, and chances are you'll meet one or more of the friendly family members. The home-cooked meals are prepared at very affordable prices. You'll eat well for under fifteen dollars. In addition to a brisk dine-in crowd, the restaurant does a big takeout business (if you are doing takeout, calling in ahead of time is recommended).

There's a crowd at lunch, chatting in English and Spanish while diving into such dishes as mofongo, a big ball of mashed plantain and garlic surrounded by your choice of sauce, such as sautéed shrimp cooked with tomatoes, onion, and green pepper or stewed chicken or meat. It's the unofficial national dish of Puerto Rico.

Everything is prepared from scratch whether you try the signature sandwich, the El Famoso "Jibarito," filled with chicken, pork, fish, or ham and cheese, with fried and flattened green plantains as the "bread" or a more traditional pollo asado con papas, roasted chicken with fried potatoes. On Thursdays, Fridays, and Saturdays, specials include salted codfish with green bananas, stewed goat, and tripe stew.

6504 Detroit Ave.
216-939-0992
rinconcriollocle.com

Left: In Spanish, Rincon is corner. Criollo usually means a happening place filled with fun, vibrant with a family atmosphere. Rincon Criollo is a corner where you feel at home.

Right: The restaurant is a popular meeting place for families and friends.

SABOR MIAMI CAFE AND GALLERY

Cuban and Latin cuisine in a charming little spot

Honduran artist Mariela Paz brings Miami flair and homestyle Latin cooking to the Old Brooklyn neighborhood, her bright and cheery little café featuring cuisine that will at least have you imagining you're in a sunny spot. She grew up in a coffee family, and both her colorful artworks and burlap coffee sacks decorate the walls, while Cuban music plays on the sound system.

Crowds line up for the crisp empanadas with traditional fillings or such creative concoctions as the La Cubana empanada filled with Cuban sandwich ingredients (roast pork, ham, cheese, and pickles); traditional Cuban sandwiches; and the Peruvian street food salchipapas (fries with sausage, corn, and cheese). For hearty appetites, there are chicken tortillas rancheras, corn tortillas topped with shredded chicken, cheese, a fried egg, ranchero sauce, and pico de gallo, and such breakfast creations as Key lime pancakes.

Coffee drinks include a Cuban Colada (sweet espresso) and Mayan Mocha (with chocolate powder and spices), both perfect for dunking churros (strips of fried dough dusted with sugar).

Paz is typically on hand in the café to add her own layer of warmth, greeting guests as if they were in her home.

4848 Broadview Rd.
440-714-0202
facebook.com/SaborMiamiCafe

Top: Honduran artist Mariela Paz created the artwork for her cheery little café, which transports guests to Miami.

Above left: The menu focuses on home-style Latin cooking.

Above right: Even the pancakes are served with tropical flair. (Photos courtesy of Sabor Miami)

SOHO CHICKEN + WHISKEY

Low Country cuisine, Tennessee whiskey, and bourbon

In this rustically trendy, little brick-walled spot, the carefully lit bar displays all sorts of amber-colored enticements, and the menu focuses on fried chicken presented with a modern take. Chefs Nolan Konkoski and Molly Smith are a married couple and not Southern (she's from Cleveland, and he's from upstate New York), but they know how to produce deep-fried perfectly crunchy fried chicken.

Both worked at other local restaurants before opening their own in Ohio City in 2011. They made some menu adjustments over the years before deciding to keep the food menu tight and focused and packed with big flavor—the perfect match for the big menu of Tennessee whiskey and bourbon.

You know you're onto something good when you dive into the complimentary fluffy biscuits, served with rosemary butter and a fruit butter and see deviled eggs on the menu—both the Classic and the more extravagant Fancy Deviled Eggs with caviar, smoked trout, and dill. For fried chicken fans, five dinner options are available, all named for times of the day. For any you can choose a boneless breast, boneless thigh, or both or a fried tofu equivalent.

The "Late Night" dinner comes with mac & cheese, collard greens, and Comeback City BBQ sauce. The "Nooner" has the accompaniments of Nashville hot sauce, avocado, potato salad, plus grilled pickles. The "Mornin'" is fried chicken served with a rosemary-infused waffle and Ohio maple syrup. Shrimp and grits (rich with bacon and lots of cheese), a half roast chicken dinner, and a Low Country boil with crab, shrimp, and kielbasa are among nonfried options. Or dive into peel-and-eat shrimp boiled with Old Bay seasoning. A side order of collards gets spicy with Cajun-style Tasso ham and a dose of red pepper flakes.

Left: SOHO serves up low country cuisine in trendy Ohio City.

Right: "Chicken n fixins" with fried chicken, deviled eggs, collard greens and coleslaw. (Photos courtesy of SOHO Chicken + Whiskey)

The Southern hospitality is as friendly as you'd expect. There's even humor at play, with the Southern-cooking Midwest chefs featuring the Carpetbagger golden lager as the house beer.

As for the rest of the booze, even the fussiest bourbon and whiskey fans will be impressed with the expansive menu that includes titillating single barrel selections (the bartenders are great at offering suggestions). You can order pours straight, with a splash or on the rocks, or in creative cocktails, such as the Blacksburg, with bourbon, sweet vermouth, Benedictine, Dr. Pepper bitters, and a pickled cherry.

The popular brunch menu includes beignets and hush puppies with gravy, plus chicken and rosemary waffles, which go perfectly with a gin fizz or a Kitchen Brew (whiskey, house-made bourbon cream, and hot coffee).

1889 W. 25th St.
216-298-9090
sohocleveland.com

SPICE KITCHEN + BAR

Farm-to-table fare flourishes

The prairie-chic aesthetic of this locavore restaurant in Cleveland's Hingtetown neighborhood at the "hinge" of the Gordon Square Arts District mirrors its raison d'etre. Farmhouse wooden tables, cut flowers, and mismatched vintage teacups enhance the look, as does a huge dining room window with sun pouring in at every angle. On the back patio outside, a server gathers fresh mint from the restaurant's herb garden for a cocktail the bartender mixes up front.

Chef Ben Bebenroth gets most of his ingredients for Spice Kitchen + Bar's harvest-driven menu from nearby farms, including the restaurant's thirteen-acre farm, Spice Acres, in Cuyahoga Valley National Park just south of Cleveland. Located in a former storefront along the trendy Detroit Shoreway directly across from popular bar Happy Dog, Spice pulls in a decidedly mixed crowd: young hipsters, aging gourmands, and a hodgepodge of folks who've read or seen the media buzz and want to sample the menu for themselves. In July 2018, Bebenroth was featured in a segment on *CBS This Morning* in which he gave a walking tour of both the farm and the restaurant. Last fall he competed on the Food Network's hit show *Chopped*.

Spice's dinner menu changes weekly and is divided into "Sharables," "Smalls," and "Substantials" and could, for example, include Killbuck Valley mushroom flatbread with caramelized onion

On-site workshops and events with Spice Catering Co. are held at Spice Acres (9570 Riverview Rd., Brecksville), one of only eleven farms in a farm-leasing scheme in Cuyahoga Valley National Park. The program is managed with the Countryside Conservancy, the only initiative in the country that conserves National Park land through sustainable farming.

Left: The menu at Spice Kitchen changes based on what is in season.

Middle: Pretty preparations feature direct-from-the-farm ingredients.

Right: The bar produces creative drinks using fresh herbs, jasmine tea and other unusual ingredients. (Photos courtesy of Spice Kitchen + Bar)

and goat cheese Gouda or tea hills smoked chicken leg with creamed Ohio corn, sautéed green beans, and beet barbeque.

The restaurant has an extensive local wine list and craft cocktails, too, which make copious use of the herb garden out back. Brunch here is a gluttonous affair with such dishes as goat cheese waffles with apple citrus compote and Dixie Benedict: crispy pork belly, hot sauce hollandaise, biscuit, sunny eggs, and hash browns. And, of course, the "Crowd Pleaser," which consists of a bottle of champagne and carafe of orange juice for make-your-own mimosas.

In addition to Burbank-based Killbuck Valley Mushrooms and Loudonville-based Tea Hills Poultry, Bebenroth works with almost two dozen other local purveyors, including Heritage Lane Farm, Quarry Hill, and James Falb Amish Dairy and Grains. Growing up in Strongsville with a mother who made regular trips to Amish country for provisions was, in fact, one of his inspirations for becoming a chef, says the ex-Marine.

5800 Detroit Ave.
216-961-9637
spicekitchenandbar.com

SETI'S POLISH BOY

Food truck serving Cleveland's iconic sandwich

The Polish Boy is a sandwich credited to Cleveland, and particularly to early barbecue joints in the city. It first appeared around the middle of the last century, and in its pure form it is grilled kielbasa on a bun, topped with French fries, BBQ sauce, and coleslaw. It is a fun mess to eat. You'll find versions on the menu at trendy eateries, but Seti's puts the sandwich front and center.

When Seti's opened in 2000, it was the city's first food truck. Chef Seti Martinez had other dishes on the menu, too, before deciding to focus on the grilled sandwiches, quarter-pound all-beef hot dogs, fries, and cold sodas, says Marsha Martinez, his wife, who is also involved in the business. Seti, who worked at many other restaurants before developing his own rolling kitchen, has had his Polish Boys featured on Food Network and the Travel Channel. Michael Symon and Andrew Zimmern of *Bizarre Foods* are among fans.

The smoked beef kielbasa is given an extra bite with a quick fry after grilling and then topped with fries and house-made BBQ sauce and coleslaw. If you want to get crazy, add on top of all that Seti's chili.

Lorain Ave. at W. 42nd St.
216-240-0745
facebook.com/setispolishboys

Top left: The Polish Boy is a Cleveland sandwich creation.

Top right: Chef Seti Martinez worked at other Cleveland restaurants before opening his popular food truck.

Above: Celebrity chefs Michael Symon and Andrew Zimmern are among fans. (Photos courtesy of Seti's Polish Boys)

XINJI NOODLE BAR

Ramen gets a local slant at this SoLo eatery

The national ramen craze took time to hit Cleveland, but this casual spot that opened in 2017 was worth waiting for. In the newly cool neighborhood, in a hip industrial space with brick walls and exposed pipes, Chef Shuxin Liu delivers deliciously well-developed flavors. His rich pork broth with black garlic simmers for some seventy-two hours.

Liu was born in China, raised in Ohio, and previously worked at local restaurants, including Momocho, as well as restaurants in New York, Seattle, and elsewhere. His menu features Northeast Ohio farm products (most of the fresh noodles are made by Sun Noodles in New Jersey). Ohio distillery products are featured in cocktails, and the beer menu has some local Ohio brews. Sake choices number about a dozen.

Diners sit at metal tables or on stools at the bar, with views of the open kitchen and Liu's graphic art (he studied graphic design at Ohio State University). The short menu features a half-dozen noodle selections, rice bowls, dumplings, and bao (steamed buns). Do not miss the amazing chicken wings, with ginger and scallion and chili sauce. Your server will provide a wet wipe, but you may want to lick every last drop of sauce from your fingers.

4211 Lorain Ave.
216-465-2439
xinjinoodle.com

Left: Chef Shuxin Liu trained as a graphic artist, and some of his work appears on the restaurant's walls.

Top right: The décor is industrial chic.

Above right: Liu delivers deliciously well-developed flavors in his ramen.

THE STANDARD

Spaetzel meets vintage urban chic

Good things happen in the open kitchen of this intimate, brick-walled bistro and bar, where the focus is modern takes on American comfort food. The big, retro marquee out front makes the place stand out in the North Collinwood neighborhood. You'd want to hang out at this local spot if you lived nearby and should seek it out of you don't. The kitchen is open until 2:00 a.m., with late-night cravings well satisfied here.

Co-owners Matt Quinn and Chris Hammer modeled the décor of their restaurant, opened in 2013, on a place owned for thirty years by Matt's father. The result is a cool vintage throwback.

The Standard does spaetzel with grilled chicken, smoked Slovenian sausage and goat cheese. Other stick-to-your ribs fare includes Gruyère mac & cheese and a short rib stroganoff with wild mushrooms. For those looking for something lighter, there are shareable "snacks," such as halloumi cheese with pickled peppers or oysters of the day served with Bloody Mary granita. The bar does wonderful interpretations of cocktails, including martinis and a classic daiquiri.

779 E. 185th St.
216-531-9643
clethestandard.com

Left: With its retro marquee, The Standard stands out in the North Collinwood neighborhood.

Top right: A butter lettuce salad gets an upgraded treatment.

Above right: Shareable snacks include grilled halloumi cheese.

BALL PARK MUSTARD

Battle of the brown mustards

Cleveland has the rare designation as home of two great brown mustards that are sometimes confused because of their names.

Bertman Original Ball Park Mustard has roots to 1925. The original mustard maker was Joseph "Joe" Bertman, an immigrant from Poland. Joe was friends with other early Cleveland food icons, such as chef Ettore Boiardi (of Chef Boyardee fame) and chef Vernon Stouffer, founder of Stouffer's. L. J. Minor, founder of what is now Nestlé, reportedly got his start working with Bertman mustard. Joe had such an influence that there's a display about Bertman Original at the local Maltz Museum of Jewish Heritage.

The slightly spicy old world–style Bertman brown mustard, grown and made in Ohio, is the official mustard of Progressive Field and baseball's professional Cleveland Indians and is available at local grocery stores, including Heinen's. It's also the main ingredient in Chef Michael Symon's barbecue sauce (see page 18).

Just don't call Bertman's mustard Authentic Stadium Mustard because that's a separate company, selling brown mustard out of Cleveland for fifty years. Ambitious salesman David Dwoskin made Stadium famous nationwide. It's sold in supermarkets around the country and is the mustard you'll find at football's professional Cleveland Browns and basketball's professional Cleveland Cavaliers games and at baseball parks around the country. It's even gone on NASA space missions.

Both brands may be ordered online.

Bertman Original Ball Park Mustard
Bertman Foods Co.
bertmanballparkmustard.com

Authentic Stadium Mustard
Davis Food Company
stadiummustard.com

Top: Joseph "Joe" Bertman, an immigrant from Poland, gained fame for his ball park mustard.

Inset: This is the old bottle label. Starting in 2019, as the Cleveland Indians remove their longtime controversial logo of Chief Wahoo from their baseball uniforms, Bertman is doing the same with its label.

RESTAURANTS A-Z

Alley Cat Oyster Bar, 2
1056 Old River Rd.

Astoria Cafe & Market, 124
5417 Detroit Ave..

Balaton Restaurant, 66
13133 Shaker Square

Ball Park Mustard, 202

Banter, 160
7320 Detroit Ave.

Bar Cento, 136
1948 West 25th St.

Barroco Arepa Bar, 70
12718 Larchmere Blvd.

Batuqui, 72
12706 Larchmere Blvd.

Big Al's Diner, 74
12600 Larchmere Blvd.

Bigmouth Donuts, 165
1418 W. 29th St.

The Black Pig, 138
2801 Bridge Ave.

Blue Point Grille, 20
700 W. St. Clair Ave.

Bratenahl Kitchen, 120
14002 Lakeshore Blvd.

Brewnuts, 164
6501 Detroit Ave.

Bruno's Ristorante, 158
2644 W. 41st St.

Butcher and the Brewer, 16
2043 E. 4th St.

Charlie's Dog House Diner, 174
2102 Brookpark Rd.

Citizen Pie, 134
15710 Waterloo Rd.
2144 W. 25th St.

Cleveland Bagel Company, 126
4201 Detroit Ave.

Collision Bend Brewing Company, 6
1250 Old River Rd.

Corbo's Bakery, 104
12210 Mayfield Rd. (Little Italy)
1603 Euclid Ave. (Playhouse Square)

Corner 11 Bowl & Wrap, 162
2391 W. 11th St.

Dante, 46
2247 Professor Ave.

Edwins, 64
13101 Shaker Square

El Rinconcito Chapin, 166
3330 Broadview Rd.

Empress Taytu, 168
6125 St. Clair Ave.

Fahrenheit, 42
2417 Professor Ave.

Farkas Pastry Shoppe, 170
2700 Lorain Ave.

Fat Cats, 44
2061 W. 10th St.

Felice, 68
12502 Larchmere Blvd.

Fire Food and Drink, 60
13220 Shaker Square

Fluffy Duck Cafe, 172
10001 Chester Ave.

The Flying Fig, 128
2523 Market Ave.

Gallucci's Italian Foods, 112
6610 Euclid Ave.

Ginko, 48
2247 Professor Ave.

Great Lakes Brewing Company, 130
2516 Market Ave.

The Greenhouse Tavern, 12
2038 E. 4th St.

Grumpy's Cafe, 52
2621 W. 14th St.

Guarino's, 176
12309 Mayfield Rd.

Hansa Brewery, 130
2717 Lorain Ave.

Happy Dog, 132
5801 Detroit Ave.

The Harp Irish Pub and Restaurant, 154
4408 Detroit Ave.

Heinen's Grocery Store Downtown Cleveland, 24
900 Euclid Ave.

Honey Hut, 182
4674 State Rd.

Hot Sauce Legacy BBQ, 110
12310 Superior Ave.

Hot Sauce Williams, 110
3770 Lee Rd.

Indian Flame, 82
11623 Euclid Ave.

Jack Frost Donuts, 165
4960 Pearl Rd.

Johnny Mango World Cafe & Bar, 152
3120 Bridge Ave.

Johnny's Bar on Fulton, 156
3164 Fulton Rd.

Johnny's Downtown, 22
1406 W. 6th St.

Johnny's Little Bar, 23
614 Frankfort Ave.

Lago Restaurant and Wine Bar, 8
1091 W. 10th St.

L'Albatros, 58
11401 Bellflower Rd.

La Plaza Supermarket and Taqueria, 178
13609 Lakewood Heights Blvd.

Larder Delicatessen and Bakery, 140
1455 W. 29th St.

Le Petit Triangle Cafe, 122
1881 Fulton Rd.

Li Wah, 76
2999 Payne Ave.

LJ Shanghai, 78
3412 Superior Ave.

Lola Bistro, 14
2058 E. 4th St.

Luca Italian Cuisine, 10
2100 Superior Viaduct

Luchita's Mexican
Restaurant, 180
3456 W. 117th St.

Lucky's Cafe, 50
777 Starkweather Ave.

Mabel's BBQ, 18
2050 E. 4th St.

Mallorca, 26
1390 W. 9th St.

Mama Santa's, 102
12301 Mayfield Rd.

Marble Room, 28
623 Euclid Ave.

Mason's Creamery, 183
4401 Bridge Ave.

Masthead Brewing Co., 131
1261 Superior Ave.

Mia Bella Restaurant, 106
12200 Mayfield Rd.

Mitchell's Ice Cream, 182
1867 W. 25th St.

Momocho Mod Mex, 142
1835 Fulton Rd.

Nate's Deli, 184
1923 W. 25th St.

Nauti Mermaid, 32
1378 W. 6th St.

Nighttown, 80
12387 Cedar Rd., Cleveland
Heights

Noble Beast Brewing Co., 130
1470 Lakeside Ave.

North Union Farmer's
Market, 62
Historic Shaker Square

Ocho Rios True Island Cuisine,
120
1007 Ivanhoe Rd.

Parallax, 40
2179 W. 11th St.

The Plum, 186
4133 Lorain Ave.

Prosperity Social Club, 38
1109 Starkweather Ave.

Pura Vida by Brandt, 30
170 Euclid Ave.

Rincon Criollo, 188
6504 Detroit Ave.

Sabor Miami Cafe and
Gallery, 190
4848 Broadview Rd.

Salt +, 144
17625 Detroit Ave., Lakewood

Seti's Polish Boy, 196
Lorain Ave. at W. 42nd St.

Siam Cafe, 114
3951 St. Clair Ave

Slyman's, 34
3106 St. Clair Ave.

SoHo Chicken + Whiskey, 192
1889 W. 25th St.

Sokolowski's University Inn, 56
1201 University Rd.

Spice Kitchen + Bar, 194
5800 Detroit Ave.

The Standard, 200
779 E. 185th St.

Superior Pho, 116
3030 Superior Ave.

Sweet Moses, 182
6800 Detroit Ave.

Szechuan Gourmet, 118
1735 E. 36th St.

Tommy's Restaurant, 108
1824 Coventry Rd., Cleveland Heights

TownHall, 150
1909 W. 25th St.

Ushabu, 54
2173 Professor Ave.

Walnut Wednesdays, 36
Chester Commons
E. 12th St. and Chester Ave.

West Side Market, 146
1979 W. 25th St.

Xinji Noodle Bar, 198
4211 Lorain Ave.

APPENDIX